Transform Yourself

A Self-hypnosis Manual

Patrick Marsolek

Inner Workings Resources LLC
Helena, Montana

Publisher's Cataloging-in-Publication
(Provided by Quality Books, Inc.)

Marsolek, Patrick.
   Transform yourself : a self-hypnosis manual / by
Patrick Marsolek.
   p. cm.
   Includes bibliographical references and index.
   LCCN 2005908121
   ISBN 0-9769041-0-1

   1. Autogenic training. 2. Hypnotism—Therapeutic
use. 3. Self-actualization (Psychology)   I. Title.

RC499.A8M65 2006   615.8'5122
                 QBI05-600146

This publication is intended to provide accurate and authoritative information on the subject matter covered. It is sold with the understanding that neither the publisher nor the author is engaged in providing professional medical or psychological services. Any use of the information in this book is at the reader's discretion. The author and publisher specifically disclaim any and all liability arising directly or indirectly from the use or application of any information contained in this book. If professional medical or psychological advice or other expert assistance is required, the services of a competent professional should be sought.

ATTENTION CORPORATIONS, UNIVERSITIES, COLLEGES, AND PROFESSIONAL ORGANIZATIONS: Quantity discounts are available on bulk purchases of this book for educational, gift purposes, or as premiums for magazine subscriptions or renewals. Special books or book excerpts can also be created to fit specific needs. For information, please contact Inner Workings Resources, PO Box 1264, Helena, MT 59624; Ph 406-443-3439

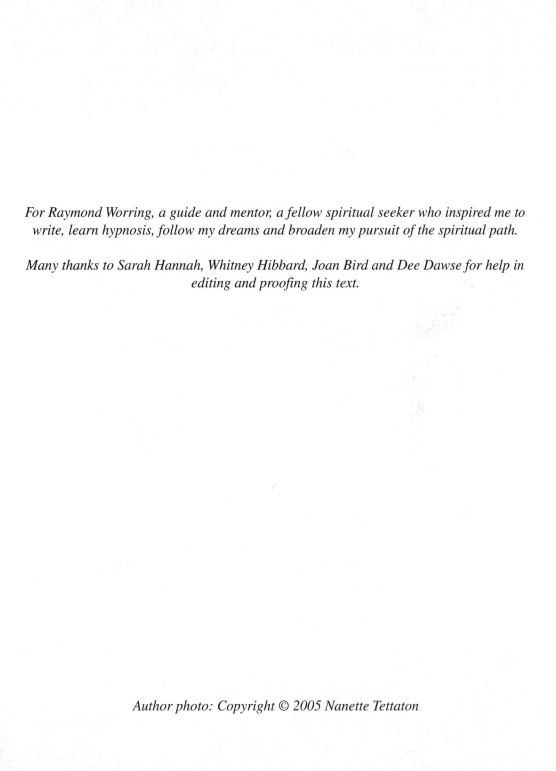

For Raymond Worring, a guide and mentor, a fellow spiritual seeker who inspired me to write, learn hypnosis, follow my dreams and broaden my pursuit of the spiritual path.

Many thanks to Sarah Hannah, Whitney Hibbard, Joan Bird and Dee Dawse for help in editing and proofing this text.

Contents

Forward

*What one believes to be true either is true or becomes true within certain limits
to be determined experimentally and experientially.
Those beliefs are to be transcended.
Lilly's Law*

Our beliefs shape our reality to a large extent. Scientific research demonstrates that what we believe influences the way we experience our world. In the human biocomputer we call the brain, our beliefs are the software that program how we experience the world. Psychology professor Charles Tart explains that our beliefs about who we are and what our world is like control our lives in many ways. If we want to change ourselves and the world we experience, we better change our beliefs.

Most of our beliefs are unconscious. We accept certain beliefs about ourselves (e.g., I'm not worthy.) and the world (e.g., Life is unfair.). If such beliefs stay in our unconscious, beyond any conscious control, they can and do affect our lives. Many of us internalize beliefs that prevent us from realizing our full potential (e.g., I can't do this job because. . .). As a result, we do not use the talent and potential we have. Astonishingly, even Einstein used only about ten percent of his mental capacity.

The good news is that self-hypnosis is a proven, effective tool for accessing and changing those unconscious and self-limiting beliefs in positive ways.

My friend and colleague, Patrick Marsolek, has written this excellent self-hypnosis guide. It will help serious readers experimentally and experientially access their unconscious, identify and transcend their self-limiting beliefs and become who they would like to be. Patrick has spent his life researching and exploring the realms of human consciousness.

Additionally, Patrick possesses a high degree of intelligence, creativity and integrity. Whatever Patrick does, he does well. This manual is no exception.

Transform Yourself offers you an invitation to guide your own personal evolution. It will help you tap into your rich inner potential and sculpt your life in the directions you desire. You will be able to access the power and creativity of your unconscious mind, your resourceful and unique ally. Enjoy the journey.

- Whitney Hibbard, Ph.D.

Introduction
Self-Hypnosis Can Help You

Who looks outside, dreams; who looks inside, awakes.
Carl Gustav Jung

Are old thought patterns, beliefs, or behaviors making your life difficult? Do you know what you want, but have a hard time making it happen? On the other hand, have you ever felt inspired or guided by an inner sense of knowing? Have you had days when you felt absolutely "on" and in control, but have no idea how to create the feeling again?

You can alter or release old, restrictive beliefs and behaviors. You can access your own creative energies and higher intelligence. Welcome to the exciting world of self-hypnosis.

Self-hypnosis is not a mysterious power limited to a few people, but an innate capacity within everyone. Self-hypnosis is a tool for personal transformation that taps into the vast resources of the subconscious mind. The subconscious is already responsible for up to 90% of your mental and physical functioning. Why not use its immense capacities to manifest your goals and dreams? You can become aware of the subconscious potentials within you and use them to transform your life. With self-hypnosis, you cut through the resistance in your conscious awareness and go to the source of your own power and wisdom. You can generate positive thoughts and ideas that have the power to change your physical body, your mind, even your whole life.

Within the practice of self-hypnosis you will learn two important skills; how to intentionally shift your awareness to a different, positive state and how to clarify and manifest a specific intention in your life.

The first skill, shifting of awareness, comes through the process of trance. Trance is a different state of mind that alters your orientation to reality. The change, whether subtle or extreme, gives you a new perspective on your life and the world around you. A new perspective isn't necessarily better than your original one, but shifting from one to the other expands your awareness and broadens your depth of experience. If your everyday state of mind is self-demeaning, dis-empowering, frustrating, or simply 'off' in some way, then shifting to another viewpoint can help you get back on track. Working with trance in self-hypnosis, you intentionally recreate another way of being that serves you better, makes you happier, and leads towards personal fulfillment.

The second major skill you learn is manifesting intention. Effective self-suggestion, visualization, and affirmation are the workhorses of the trance experience. In trance, the ideas, images and feelings you bring to mind literally move you into the experience of your goals and dreams. When you bring an intention to mind, your heart, body, mind and spirit all respond. The suggestions you give yourself send ripples of change out to the farthest, deepest corners of your being. Then, as you return to your normal state, your intentions continue working at a subconscious level, manifesting in delightful and surprising ways. Both the ability to shift your awareness and the ability to manifest your intention will have far-reaching effects in your life. You will discover the uses and benefits of these abilities throughout the course of this book, and experience the rewards of self-hypnosis for yourself.

As you practice, learn, and use self-hypnosis, you will start living your life the way you dream or imagine. You can have the ease, peace and well-being you know are possible. You can change your reality! Even if you don't consciously know what changes you need to make, your own inner intelligence will guide you in the right direction. In trance, you come in touch with a larger, wiser part of your being, whether called a "higher self," "collective unconscious" or "spirit."

Is the kind of transformation I'm talking about with self-hypnosis real? As a teacher of self-hypnosis and as a clinical hypnotherapist, I've seen many dramatic changes. Here's a testimonial from one of my clients:

> Hypnotherapy has been a wonderful experience for me and I strongly believe it could help a majority of people. I am not the type of person that comes to mind when people think of hypnosis. I tend to be very analytical and straightforward, hence my profession - a computer support technician. I came to Patrick skeptical but hopeful he could help me with a phobia I have. I tried the more 'traditional' methods (i.e. counseling, medication) but with no success. After a few appointments with Patrick, my phobia has dramatically diminished and I anticipate triumph. It has been a great tool

for me even though I have no idea how it works.

The most amazing thing has happened to me while using hypnosis to overcome my phobia. I have found myself more self assured, happier, and less stressed during my day-to-day life. For example, I lost control of my car while driving on the icy interstate. While my car was spinning in circles and eventually went into the ditch, my mind replayed the positive messages Patrick had said during some of our sessions. Instead of panicking (among other things!), I calmly thought of what my options were and no matter what, I would be okay because I can always take care of myself. These suggestions were casually said during our sessions. There are numerous examples I can give for the positive affects hypnosis has had but this tends to be the most extreme.

Sincerely, Deb

There also is hard data proving the effectiveness of hypnosis and self-hypnosis. Researchers at Beth Israel Deaconess Hospital in Boston conducted a randomized study of the effectiveness of hypnosis in easing pain and anxiety associated with minimally invasive surgeries. (Lang, et al., 2000) Patients were divided into several groups, one of which received hypnosis. The results indicated procedures took less time for the hypnosis group and less than half the medication was used. In the hypnosis group, blood pressure and heart rate did not increase or decrease to levels of concern. Lastly, pain and anxiety were rated lowest by patients in the hypnosis group throughout the surgery and continuing into their recovery.

The hypnosis group experienced these results through a simple hypnotic technique of focusing on the breath and concentrating on the sensation of floating. They also directed their attention towards a "safe and comfortable" place. This last suggestive phrase did have tangible, immediate results for the patients; they reported feeling much more comfortable than the control group. The patients' use of hypnosis positively affected their reality; their surgical experience became safer and more comfortable.

In other studies (Dossey, 2000), hypnosis was shown to be up to 90% effective in treating congenital ichthyosis, a genetic skin disease which has no known cure and is characterized by excessive scales. Hypnosis may be able to transform our physical bodies down to the genetic level! These medical examples show us how hypnosis can have a positive effect on our bodies.

Mickey, a former student of mine, had a heart attack. She made it safely to the ER where the doctors performed an angioplasty, which involved putting a balloon and stent into her artery. Mickey's daughter called me shortly after her procedure to help ease her pain. I worked with her for approximately 30 minutes in her hospital room, guiding her into trance and giving her suggestions to feel more comfortable and calm. Two weeks later, she sent me a note:

May 4, 2004

Hi Patrick,

I cannot thank you enough for helping me on April 16th. The pains in my chest were severe and the cardiologist told me they usually lasted a few weeks! I couldn't be given any pain killer except morphine (due to extreme allergies) and I was receiving only occasional drips from an I.V. But within just a few minutes under hypnosis the pain vanished - never to return!! The nurses were mystified by all this - and asked many questions. Mountains of thanks.

Lovingly, Micki

Since I had worked with Mickey before, she responded very favorably. Fortunately for her, she thought of hypnosis as a tool when other options for relief weren't available.

There are peer-reviewed studies showing how hypnosis and self-hypnosis are effective with the following conditions: habit coughing in children, pain control, childbirth, chronic fatigue, irritable bowel syndrome, and anxiety. Hypnosis has also been shown to be effective for relieving stress and trauma, building optimism, losing weight, getting rid of nervous tics and habits, and helping students pass exams. If you want to read more on the effectiveness of hypnosis, I've included the sources in Appendix E. I won't go further into substantiating hypnosis in this manual. The purpose of this book is to give you first-hand experience with the transformative power of hypnosis.

This manual will take you through a series of graduated steps, introducing you to self-hypnosis. After each exercise you will have an opportunity to evaluate your experience and decide how meaningful each technique is for you. Learning self-hypnosis is a "hands-on" process with simple, practical exercises.

You will learn what self-hypnosis is, how to use it effectively, and how to apply its transformative power in your life. You will learn the mechanics of hypnosis, which can be broken down into four basic parts:

Induction - The process you use to intentionally shift your awareness into a hypnotic state of mind. For example, you might pay attention to your breathing. Then, as your breath starts to slow down, you feel your body relaxing.

Deepening - Any intentional process taking you further into your experience of hypnosis. This might involve something simple like imagining a stairway and walking yourself "down" into a more comfortable feeling.

Use of Trance (Auto-suggestions) - Using a script of specific words and phrases which addresses your intentions. Auto-suggestions are either read completely in trance, or activated with a specific key phrase, key words or image. This is also the phase where the workings of the subconscious are more accessible and other trance explorations can occur.

Awakening - A brief, formal process whereby you return to your normal state of consciousness and exit the hypnotic state.

You will learn how inductions and deepenings work and how to write and use an effective auto-suggestion. Working consciously on your auto-suggestion while practicing self-hypnosis creates an effective bridge between your conscious and subconscious mind. Your own personal auto-suggestion will be highly effective in and out of trance; it can and will transform you.

Throughout this manual, I will include comments from students who have taken my classes. The purpose is to give you a greater sense of perspective for your own experiences. Since self-hypnosis is an internal process, we only know it from our own experience. We experience things differently. For example, here are some general comments from students who have had several weeks of practice in the beginners' class:

> "I've felt a more positive approach to my life, higher ability to shift my focus, and have a smoother relationship with my coworkers, husband, and children. I have more self-awareness of my moods and confidence in my life path."

> "The best part for me, is that my meditations have greatly improved. I have felt, in my daily life, that my intention has already created a large shift in me. There are several important things coming together now."

There are many unexpected benefits to using self-hypnosis. The woman above who found her meditations improving wasn't even focusing on that aspect of her life. This was a welcome side-effect. As you begin learning self-hypnosis, you will expand your awareness of yourself. You can focus specifically on an important issue. You can use self-hypnosis effectively to quit smoking, lose weight, relieve stress and tension, manage chronic pain, access creativity and intuition, improve study habits, increase your learning power, gain control over unconscious habits, create new healthy ways of being, and much more. Whatever your intention, you can experience tangible results. You can attain your goals much easier when the conscious and subconscious parts of your mind are working together.

The material in this guide has evolved out of my personal inquiry into trance and the exploration of my own consciousness. I also work as a clinical hypnotherapist, write and research on consciousness, and teach classes in self-hypnosis, trance, intuition and remote viewing. After many years of exploration, I continue to be enriched by my experiences with hypnosis. In this manual, I hope to share what I've learned and inspire in you the same sense of fascination and excitement I feel towards self-hypnosis. I also look forward to many more years of learning.

There is nothing mysterious about self-hypnosis. Once you learn the mechanics of it, you will be able to adapt every aspect of its structure to suit your personal needs. You will be able to use self-hypnosis effectively to take care of yourself, feel empowered, and change your life. This skill, once learned, will remain with you the rest of your life.

Using this manual

This manual proceeds through a specific series of hands-on, practical exercises. Each exercise is important, building on the previous ones, and providing you with another piece of the process. I've included some theory to give you a working framework to understand what self-hypnosis is. Having a cognitive understanding of hypnosis is important; only when you know you will be safe will you allow yourself to 'let go' and experience hypnosis effectively.

There are also guided hypnosis inductions for several of the exercises on the accompanying CD. You will use these inductions at specific points as you go through the workbook. They are intended to supplement your own self-hypnosis practice. I recommend using a portable CD player with stereo headphones to listen to these tracks. This way you can listen easily in whatever comfortable position you choose.

If you've had experience with guided inductions and visualizations, you may want to listen to the CD tracks independently. If you do this without the accompanying self-practice, you won't benefit as much from them. Be patient and work your way through the chapters. The complete script for each exercise on the CD is in the text. You can read each script afterwards to refresh your conscious mind as to what occurred. Reread parts you enjoyed and integrate them into your own practice.

Each exercise lists any materials needed and has a time recommendation with it. Allow yourself the full time required to gain the full benefits of the exercise. If you don't have enough time to do the exercise without feeling rushed, then wait until you can give each exercise your full attention.

Every exercise also has follow-up questions for you to answer regarding your experiences. Have a journal or notebook handy to work through each of the questions. Thinking and writing about your experiences is an important part of learning self-hypnosis. Consciously addressing and describing what you thought or felt will help you acknowledge what you are learning and help you understand which tools work best for you. Writing will help you effectively integrate your conscious awareness with the subconscious processes of hypnosis. The time recommendations include the time needed for the follow-up questions.

Typically, I teach the course of learning outlined in this book in a four-week, evening class. This gives participants ample time to practice, experience, and receive feedback from me and the other participants. I recommend that you also take your time working your way through the book. Feel free to repeat each of the exercises presented here, to gain the full benefits. Give yourself time between each of the exercises to process your experiences. Approximately half way through the book, I've included a homework practice form. When you reach this point, you will have an understanding of the basic mechanics of self-hypnosis. Be sure to take some time at some point to get in some personal practice sessions in and review the earlier parts of the book.

This manual can be done in a group or individually. If you are working with a group or class setting, the inductions can be experienced together and discussed as a group. Sharing experiences is helpful, because each person gains a better understanding of the range of responses possible with each exercise.Whether you work in a group or alone, your learning happens inside your experience.

Let's begin!

change your reality

Chapter 1
Beliefs about hypnosis

There is no need to go to India or anywhere else to find peace. You will find that deep place of silence right in your room, your garden or even your bathtub.
Elisabeth Kubler-Ross

Self-hypnosis entrance

Self-hypnosis is essentially an inner, subjective experience. You will experience self-hypnosis in your own unique way, depending on your personality, what interests you, how you live in your mind and body, and many other variables. As you work your way through this manual, you will come to understand what hypnosis means for you. Recognizing and validating your own experience is essential to using hypnosis effectively.

Your beliefs about hypnosis, and all aspects relating to hypnosis, determine how you experience it. If you have apprehension about some aspect of hypnosis, say from something you've seen in a movie or on a stage, you will hold back from allowing yourself to have the experience. Unrealistic expectations also can get in the way of your progress. Before beginning, I will address common concerns to help you feel safe and comfortable. You can experience self-hypnosis in a way that is right for you.

Discovering what your beliefs are and looking at them consciously will help you move past any obstacles to your progress. It is helpful to understand fears or expectations you have about hypnosis. So, before I say more about what self-hypnosis is, I'd like to help you become more aware of the beliefs you already have.

Belief Questionnaire

Materials Needed - Journal
Time - 20 - 30 minutes.

Answer the following questions in your journal. (You can rewrite the questions if you want them for later reference.) This isn't a test. There are no right or wrong answers. These questions are only for your self-awareness. Take your time and put some thought into your answers. Be thorough and honest with yourself.

1 - What is hypnosis?

2 - Is self-hypnosis different than hypnosis? If so, how?

3 - If you have experienced hypnosis or self-hypnosis, what are your thoughts and feelings about your experience?

4 - Have you ever observed hypnosis or self-hypnosis? If so, what were your thoughts or reactions?

5 - Is there anything dangerous about hypnosis or self-hypnosis?

6 - Why do you want to learn self-hypnosis?

7 - What do you expect the experience of self-hypnosis to be like? Be specific.

8 - Does it take special skills or talents to experience or use self-hypnosis effectively? If so, what?

9 - Do you think you will be a good subject? Why?

10 - What is the subconscious?

11 - Can you trust your subconscious? Explain.

12 - Describe a place, a time, or a memory, where you felt safe, comfortable and empowered. This can be real or imaginary. Describe all the feelings and senses you experienced at this place.

Discussion of beliefs

I purposely started with this questionnaire before giving you more information about hypnosis. This way, you have a record of your beliefs before taking on any new ones. After experiencing self-hypnosis, you can revisit your answers to see if your beliefs have shifted.

I will address some of the above questions to provide more information about hypnosis and self-hypnosis. Since hypnosis is essentially a subjective, inner experience, no one else can tell you exactly what it will be like for you. Even the experts don't agree on what hypnosis is. (See Appendix A for some different definitions.) If I offer an explanation of some aspect of hypnosis or trance and it doesn't fit with your experience, stop for a moment. Pay attention to your feelings. Even though you may consider yourself a beginner, honor your sense of what is right. If an exercise feels a little strange or awkward, give it a try. You can review it critically and objectively afterwards. You can decide if and how each technique might be meaningful.

1. What is hypnosis?

Hypnosis is a process that intentionally utilizes our natural ability to go into trance, to access the subconscious, and to create positive changes in our lives.

I'll elaborate on this definition, starting with the word, trance. Trance is an altered state of consciousness. You experience a trance any time you focus your awareness in such a way that your normal orientation to reality changes or shifts. Trance is something everyone experiences naturally. When you lay down to sleep at night, you shift your awareness inward. You focus on the feelings in your body, your memories of the day, or your thoughts and feelings. As your focus shifts, you lose touch with the world around you and eventually fall asleep. You may not pay much attention to this transitional state in between waking and sleeping, also called the hypnagogic state, but it is one of the most common trance states.

If driving your regular route to work and suddenly you find yourself at the exit or turnoff without realizing "where" you've been, you've experienced a trance. While you were driving, you might have been thinking about what you had to do for the day, what happened the night before, or even recalling a conversation you had with a friend. Whatever you were thinking shifted your orientation inwards and you lost touch with the world around you. I like this example because it also shows us how even in trance, we have an inner intelligence taking care of us. We continue driving the right speed, stay in the right lane, and we "wake up" when we reach our exit. (You can override this wisdom in dangerous ways when you are overtired or on drugs.)

Spontaneous trancing also occurs when you find yourself daydreaming during a boring lecture or when you're absorbed in a good book or movie and lose track of the time. These are all examples of natural, spontaneous trances. (See the flowchart on page 147, for a visual representation of how we move through trances each day and how they are helpful to us.)

Hypnosis is a process that uses trance intentionally. Once you realize how you go in and out of natural trance states, you can start using them to serve your awareness and intention.

2. Is self-hypnosis different than hypnosis?

Many people learn how to experience hypnosis with a hypnotherapist as a guide. These people are trained to work with trance and understand the mechanics of the process. They know how trancing occurs, how to induce it, and how to use it effectively. But since we all experience natural trances, all it takes to experience hypnosis is to use our natural trancing ability intentionally. Many professionals using hypnosis believe all hypnosis is essentially self-hypnosis. At some level, even in a therapeutic setting, the subject agrees or chooses to go into trance. The hypnotist or hypnotherapist simply serves as a guide to facilitate the process, and assists in navigating the trance state.

It's generally easier to go into trance with someone you trust as a guide. If you don't trust your guide (either yourself or someone else), you won't experience hypnosis. Having said this, your experience of hypnosis can be very different than self-hypnosis. In heterohypnosis (hypnosis with another person) with someone you trust, you can "let go" to a greater degree because you won't need to reserve a part of your awareness to guide the experience. In self-hypnosis, you act as both the guide and the experiencer; you lead yourself into the trance state.

Though some people experience a deeper sense of trance when guided, self-hypnosis has its advantages. Knowing how to alter your conscious awareness for positive purposes is inherently empowering. When you transform yourself through your own personal process, there can be no doubt it is your ability that facilitates the change. In self-hypnosis there's no room to believe you are giving away your power to anyone else. Thus, self-hypnosis can be more effective for certain issues, especially with building self-esteem and self-confidence.

3. Thoughts and feelings about your hypnotic experiences.

Have you ever imagined a happy place as a way of "escaping" for a little while? Your escape induces a trance for a specific intention - to feel better. Your intentional trance is self-hypnosis. Hypnosis is a more formalized process but can include spontaneous trances that serve you.

It's important to be aware how you feel about the experiences you've had. If you are critical of yourself or feel guilty for "spacing out" or "not being productive," then you may want to reconsider the value of your experiences.

Entering 'trance' allows your subconscious processes to return to a natural balance, much the same way your body rests and restores itself when you sleep. A little 'trancing out' in the middle of a busy work day helps your brain get rest and rejuvenation. You can return from self-hypnosis or a short nap feeling more energized and refreshed. You may also find you're more able to focus on your work after such a break.

It's easy to discount the experience of trance because it may not be as logical as the rest of your life. If you enjoyed a brief nap or visualization in the afternoon, then awakened feeling refreshed and energized, congratulate yourself. You already know how self-hypnosis can be helpful.

4. Thoughts and feelings about observing hypnosis.

Public display of hypnosis usually only occurs in the field of entertainment. You may have seen stage shows at a fair, a convention, or even at a night-club. These presentations portray a very authoritarian style of hypnosis, where the hypnotist controls his subjects and makes them do strange things. This style is used to create fast, flashy responses and is in complete contrast to the more permissive, client-centered style used in hypnotherapy. I like to point out how even at these shows, subjects still choose what they want to experience. There are always some who don't respond and are sent from the stage. Those on stage often go along with the hypnotist for the sake of the show, though some people are very sucseptible and do have geniune hypnotic experiences.

Hollywood portrays hypnosis in a variety of ways, which are also somewhat skewed. To keep viewers from becoming hypnotized, large portions of the induction process are left out of film. Then subjects are shown having scary or uncontrolled experiences. This may lead you to expect immediate and unrealistic results and that hypnosis isn't safe.

Whatever hypnotic demonstrations you've observed, keep in mind the context of the demonstration. Hypnosis for entertainment is just that. It is always skewed to make you, the viewer, respond in a certain way. These demonstrations play on common misconceptions about hypnosis that I will cover next.

5. Is there anything dangerous about hypnosis or self-hypnosis?

Pay close attention to your answers to this question. Your fears about hypnosis will influence how you experience it. If you don't feel safe with hypnosis, you won't experience it in a meaningful way. So, let's look at some of the common misconceptions.

Losing control is a common misconception. Hypnosis is not about losing or giving away control. As I mentioned with the car-driving example, even in trance there is a deeper part of you always in control. Your inner intelligence is always looking out for you. In hypnosis and self-hypnosis, your subconscious is always in control. (Current research on the subconscious shows conscious control is more an illusion than we like to believe.) In hypnosis you allow your subconscious to take care of everything it normally does anyhow. By welcoming it, you allow yourself to turn over conscious control to a trusted ally who is always looking out for you. If you're driving in a bit of a trance and a child steps out into the street, you become instantly aware and react appropriately. The only time this is not the case is when you are overly tired or under the influence of a drug. At those times you shouldn't be driving!

Even while working with a hypnotist or hypnotherapist, you always have the ability to choose which suggestions feel right. No matter how deep a trance you experience, you are always in control. You can take care of yourself. Even the strange antics of people in a stage hypnotist's show are appropriate to the situation. These people have agreed to have these experiences in this setting. If for any reason they didn't want to, or they didn't feel safe, they wouldn't do it. The next time you see such an act, pay attention to those who are dismissed from the stage. They've made their choice not to respond to the hypnotist's suggestions.

I'll get stuck in hypnosis. I believe this misconception comes from Hollywood's portrayal of hypnosis, which is often based on lack of control. Like any other state of consciousness, you will only stay in trance as long as it's beneficial to you and serves you in some way. In this aspect, hypnosis is like sleep. You only sleep as long as your body needs rest. Yet, even when tired, you can consciously choose to stay awake if you need to. You can always choose when it's the right time for you to enter trance, if it's appropriate, and how long you want your experience to last.

Low intelligence. Some messages from the older, authoritarian models of hypnosis still linger. For some time, hypnosis was assumed to be the force of one strong will over another, implying the subject was inferior in some way or of lower intelligence. However, research has shown how people of all degrees of intelligence can respond to hypnosis and benefit from it. (The exception would be individuals with extremely low mental functioning.) Increasing your knowledge of hypnosis is one of the best ways to alleviate fears or misconceptions and is your best bet for success. Allowing yourself to experience a healthy trance is a sign of greater intelligence and understanding. You always have the choice stay in control in your hypnotic trance and you always decide what's right for you.

Gullibility. There is a fear that being hypnotized means you are gullible and easily swayed, or that you become more easily deceived. Herein lies one of the key differences of modern theraputic use of trance which is client centered. As your subconscious guides you in trance, you gain more control over your life. You choose what you want to be receptive and open to, and you cease giving away control to others.

Suggestibility. Hypnosis uses suggestibility to create change. Suggestibility is an openness to an idea that resonates with you. Whenever you learn something, you open to the ideas or information you are interested in. With intentional conscious use of trance, you become less suggestible to unconscious deception and more responsive to ideas, information, and people who are meaningful to you. You choose what fits for you.

6. Why do you want to learn self-hypnosis?

Answering this question starts you on the path toward change. Simply stating an intention activates a process in your subconscious. It is important, though, to understand that hypnosis is not a cure-all. It isn't a mysterious force to make all your problems magically disappear, but is a very powerful process whereby you make tremendous changes in your life. Self-hypnosis is about taking control and owning your innate power through self-understanding, self-awareness, and practice.

7. What do you expect self-hypnosis to be like?

Your expectations of self-hypnosis are very important. They will tend to lead the nature of your experiences. You may have expectations that are influenced by what you've seen in the movies or on stage. I commonly hear clients say they weren't hypnotized, even after they've manifested many of the phenomena of hypnosis. Their reasoning is that they heard me the whole time. They expected to be unconscious. Another common belief is that they won't be able to move their body. This response, also called catalepsy, only occurs in a deep trance, and only if the subject is open to the experience. If you expect to be in control, empowered and aware, you will be.

Remember times when you may have spontaneously entered a light trance, perhaps before drifting to sleep or while daydreaming. What you experienced then will often be similar to your hypnotic state. You may have interesting body sensations, feel a calmness, a lightness, or a heaviness in your body, or may even have lost awareness of one or two of your senses. These are common responses and can be welcomed when they occur as indications of trance.

8. Does it take any special skills or talents to be able to experience or use self-hypnosis effectively?

Hypnosis is a skill you can learn. It requires a desire, a willingness to learn, and persistence. The more you practice, the more you will understand yourself and how your consciousness works. It is easier for some than others. Like musical or mathematical ability, some people have a natural talent. Regardless how much hypnotic "talent" you have, you can learn to use self-hypnosis effectively..

9. Do you think you will be a good hypnotic subject?

You can become a good hypnotic subject. Studies of "hypnotic susceptibility" indicate 80% have some hypnotic ability and perhaps 10% to 15% are highly "susceptible." Methods of testing for hypnotic ability invariably rely on certain types of induction techniques. Since we're all different, we respond differently to these techniques. Because we all experience natural trance states, I believe everyone who wants to can learn to use self-hypnosis. As you go through this manual, you will have the opportunity to experiment with different techniques for inducing trance. If one doesn't work for you, try another. Keep trying until you find one that feels right.

If you are analytical, you may need to practice relaxing your critical mind. Because the analytical, critical thinking processes are more strongly associated with the conscious mind, you need to learn to relax your conscious awareness in order to build a connection to the subconscious. To experience trance, it's important to allow yourself to become absorbed in feelings, images and sensations. When you begin the exercises, give yourself permission to relax the inner critic for the duration of the exercise. Afterwards, decide for yourself if your experience has been meaningful or helpful.

10. What is the subconscious?

Simply put, the subconscious comprises everything that is in some way connected to your mind, body, heart and spirit but isn't in your conscious awareness. The subconscious isn't a static region of the brain. It constantly changes as the content of your conscious awareness changes. For instance, the sensations in the bottom of your right foot were probably not conscious until you read this sentence. The same may be true regarding awareness of your breath. These sensations come in and out of your consciousness with the flow of your attention. The speed of your breath is being controlled by your subconscious, at least until you attend to it. You can bring your breath into conscious awareness and change how you breathe once you focus your attention there.

Within your subconscious are bits of information, knowledge, and processes, some of which you can access, some you can't, and some you aren't even aware of. Current research indicates that the subconscious has more control of our lives than our limited conscious awareness does.

All of your conscious experiences that have become memory and other learned behaviors also reside in the subconscious. When you learned to drive a car, you had to consciously attend to the mechanics of the process; shifting, clutching, braking, steering, seeing, and even tracking the feeling of movement. All of this, once learned, moved into the subconscious where it functions like a computer program. Your driving program starts up every time you get behind the wheel. You don't need to consciously register all of the elements. In fact, if you tried to track all the variables of driving you would probably become too confused to drive safely.

The subconscious also contains processes and information that have never been conscious, such as feelings, thoughts, and information you physically perceived but didn't consciously register. All the unconscious mechanisms of your body and mind that you are unable to consciously perceive are also part of the subconscious. You can reduce your blood pressure without understanding what causes it. You don't need to know what the mechanism is or what needs to be changed. You only need to know what result you want. Even instinctual "programming" hard-wired into your genes is part of your subconscious and can be influenced through hypnosis.

Whatever you call it -- higher consciousness, spirit, the collective unconscious or creativity -- your subconscious includes a connection to your 'higher' potentials. You can access these parts to receive intuition, gain deeper spiritual insight, and discover new creative solutions or inventions.

11. Can you trust your subconscious?

Your answer to this question will reveal beliefs about hypnosis and the subconscious. If you believe you can't trust your subconscious, then it is important to understand the reasons why. I'm not going to tell you you should; it's up to you to decide. I have found though, as I have gained more trust in my subconscious, my experience of hypnosis has become more and more valuable. My overall self-trust has increased. I have learned the subconscious is a malleable, flexible part of my being. I can and do work with it.

When people fear the subconscious, it is often because they view it as primal and regressive. This can be the case if we are truly cut off from ourselves and our deeper emotions and feelings. For instance, if you were taught anger was not an appropriate emotion, then you may not consciously recognize when you are feeling anger. Since these feelings are repressed, they may surface any time you loosen your conscious control, as in dreams, daydreams, or the hypnotic state. Psychologists tell us that we all have these "shadow" parts of ourselves to greater or lesser degrees.

As you learn to use hypnosis and your connection to the subconscious more intentionally, you will re-own deeper parts of yourself and become more healthy and balanced. Through the gentle, step-by-step practice of learning self-hypnosis, you will become more integrated. There may be uncomfortable parts in your subconscious, but there is also a tremendous intelligence. Your subconscious is already guiding you and taking care of you. Think about the part of you that tells you it's time to sleep when you are hungry, or generates a feeling of loneliness when you need companionship. You trust these subconscious perceptions. Even when discomfort arises, you welcome your feelings as part of the process of self-discovery and healing.

As you work your way through this manual, continue to be aware of your responses to the exercises and ideas. If something doesn't feel right, take a moment to pay attention to your feelings. Write down and describe what you're feeling and see if you can tell what made you uncomfortable. Your uncomfortable response may reveal deeper beliefs or assumptions you hold to be true. Being aware of these assumptions will help you consciously understand them.

12. Describe a safe place.

The reason I had you describe a safe, comfortable place was to start activating your unconscious mind through your imagination. Thinking about this real or imaginary place takes your body into the feeling and memories of that place. It changes the way you feel. Any time you bring to mind a place or a time like this, you can shift the way you are feeling to one more comfortable and empowered. That is an easy way into a healthy trance, through your imagination. This question wasn't really about beliefs; rather it starts moving you into a positive trance. How did thinking and describing this place make you feel? You can use that feeling when you want to, and you will use it again later in this manual.

I've addressed the initial questions about hypnosis, trance and the subconscious. Now you can begin to explore trance for yourself, first with your imagination.

Chapter 2
Mind-Body Connection

The universe is transformation; our life is what our thoughts make it.
Marcus Aurelius

Exercise one - heavy/light hands

Imagination is one of the most effective paths to the subconscious. With this exercise, you will explore the connection between your mind and body using imagination. As with all the exercises in this book, you always have the choice to do or not do whatever is suggested. Give yourself permission to experience suggestion; allow yourself to learn from some new experiences.

Sit in a chair for this exercise. Then listen to Exercise One on the audio CD. There is a short introduction on the CD which you can also listen to before you begin. When you're finished with the exercise, fill out the questionnaire on page 33 and 34.

If you don't have the audio CD for this workbook and if you have a partner or a friend assisting you with these exercises, instruct them to read the following script for you. For all the scripts in this manual, read the words slowly and with intention. Let your voice relax. Pause a few moments at the end of each sentence to allow the words to settle in. As you read, enjoy the sound of the words as well as their meanings. This allows your subconscious to respond directly to the suggestions in the text.

If you are at all worried about losing control, repeat this exercise while resisting the suggestions. Knowing you can stay in control, when you want to, is important. Any time you experience something uncomfortable, you can simply stop, open your eyes, let go of what you're imagining, and reorient yourself to the room around you. You can take care of yourself. You can always decide what is right for you. If other fears arise, pay attention to them. Acknowledge your fears and address them. You can and should feel safe and in control before continuing.

Introduction to the mind/body connection - CD exercise #1
Materials needed - CD and portable player, journal
Time - 30 minutes (Includes time for follow-up questions.)

Heavy/light hands script:

> To begin, I'd like you to sit upright in a comfortable chair so you can breathe deeply and easily.
> As you sit comfortably, take a deep breath in . . . and exhale all the way out.
> Do this again, nice deep breath in . . . and out.
> Now I'd like you to extend both your arms straight out in front of you with your palms facing down.
> If you can't do this, then just imagine your arms are out in front of you.
> Close your eyes and continue breathing easily and naturally and listen to the sound of my voice.
> I'd like you to imagine the handle of a thick, plastic bucket just beneath your left hand.
> Let your hand close around the handle.
> Then imagine someone turning on a faucet just above the bucket and letting a stream of water flow into the bucket, starting to fill it up.
> You may see the bucket and the flowing water in your mind's eye.
> You may feel its weight beginning to pull your hand down . . . and you may also hear the sound of the water splashing into the bucket.
> Enjoy these senses however you imagine them.
> As you do this, your whole arm will start to get heavy.
> You can allow that feeling, you don't have to resist it.
> Your arm may even begin to move in response.
> At the same time, I want you to imagine that there's a string looped around the palm of your right hand.
> This string goes up to a bright helium balloon that's filling up, getting larger and larger,

pulling your hand up gently.

However you imagine this, enjoy it.

You may even see the color of the balloon getting brighter.

What color is it?

You may feel the string pulling up stronger on your hand.

You may hear the sound of the balloon expanding as the helium rushes in.

With each breath you breathe . . . easily and naturally . . . imagine the bucket with the water getting heavier and heavier.

Imagine the balloon getting lighter and lighter.

Allow and enjoy all these sensations.

You can allow your feelings to flow into your body.

You don't have to resist anything you're experiencing.

You can allow your hands and arms to move as they want.

You can hear the sounds . . . feel the feelings in your hands, arms, and shoulders . . . and see those images clearer and clearer.

Enjoy these sensations for a few more moments.

Then, allowing those senses to stay with you, I'd like you to open your eyes and notice where your hands and arms are now.

Then let go of the images and allow your arms to drop down into your lap.

Let your body return to normal.

This is the end of this exercise.

Turn off the CD and answer the questions in the manual.

End Script

Personal responses

Now take a few moments while this experience is fresh in your mind and answer these questions in your journal;

1 - What was the position of your arms when you opened your eyes?

2 - Was this position surprising or interesting to you in some way? How?

3 - What changes or sensations did you experience in your mind or body during this exercise?

4 - What do you think caused the changes you felt?

5 - What emotions did you feel during or after this exercise?

6 - What was the most interesting part of this exercise for you?

7 - What was the most difficult or frustrating part of this exercise?

8 - Which senses did you find the easiest to imagine?

9 - Which senses did you have difficulty imagining?

10 - Was any part of this exercise uncomfortable?

Discussion

This first exercise explores the connection between your mind and your body. If you bring an image or an idea to mind, there will be a response in your body. The degree to which you allow yourself to imagine something, determines the strength of response. Your mind and body are intimately connected. Imagining the bucket and the balloon is a simple technique used by hypnotherapists to determine how responsive a person is to suggestion. For your purposes though, it's not as important how much arm movement you had as becoming aware of what was easy and what was difficult. We all imagine differently, relying more on one sense and less on another. The purpose of this exercise is to give you more awareness of how your imagination works and what feels comfortable to you.

If, when you opened your eyes, your right hand was higher than your left, then you successfully allowed the suggestions. Your body responded. Congratulate yourself. Imagination may be fairly easy for you. You can use your imagination very effectively as you learn self-hypnosis. Be aware though, if things come too easy for you, you may not discipline yourself. Be sure to keep practicing!

It's okay if your hands were in the same position at the end as when you started. This response indicates you are in control. You decide what happens in your body. Pay particular attention to what you experienced. Did you feel a lightness or heaviness, but not allow your arms to move? If so, ask yourself why. You may have had a fear of losing control, or a fear of experiencing something unknown. If you felt some fear, or just a little resistance, remind yourself that allowing the responses and sensations in your body is okay. You aren't losing control when you allow things to happen. You are shifting control to a different part of your being, to your subconscious, much like when you go to sleep each night. Remember, you can always maintain conscious control when you need to.

If your hands didn't move, you may have been expecting something 'else' to come in and take over. You may have felt that by allowing your hands to move you would have interfered with what was supposed to happen. Sometimes you will feel the subconscious actually moving your body without your conscious control, like when you are very tired and can't keep your eyes open. More often though, the movements of the subconscious are more subtle. Within the context of this exercise, you can allow the arms to move when they start to feel heavy. Letting go is partly conscious and partly not. Even if you think you are consciously involved in the movement of the arms, you can allow it to happen. You send a message to your subconscious how you are willing to let it lead.

If your hands didn't move and you didn't feel any difference between the arms, you may have some resistance to using your imagination. Perhaps you thought the exercise was stupid or silly. You may even have heard a voice in your head telling you so. If so, then you might want to reconsider imagination and what value it has for you. Remember how imagining a safe place had a very real effect for patients undergoing surgery. Also, your ability to imagine allows you to try things out in your mind before doing them in reality. We all use our imagination in many, many ways, every single day. Inventors use imagination to come up with new ideas. Athletes use imagination to 'see' the right move or action before they do it. You already use your imagination to get a sense of the right food to eat at a meal, to rehearse a conversation you are going to have with a loved one, or to figure out the best route to drive to a store.

In hypnosis, imagination opens a connection to the subconscious. You may not consciously know how to slow your heart rate. There is no dial to turn, but imagining a dial in your imagination, and slowing turning it, can slow your heart rate. Imagining a pleasant scene on a beach can generate the same result. Imagining a safe place can lessen the pain you're experiencing. If you had difficulty imagining the bucket or the balloon, your beliefs about imagination may be getting in your way. Tell yourself imagination is okay and can have tangible results.

If you couldn't see the bucket, the water, or the balloon, you may not be a visual thinker. Focus on the senses that you can easily imagine. If your arms didn't move, or moved very little, I'd like you to repeat this exercise. Tell yourself it's okay to allow the feelings and responses to happen and remind yourself you are always in control. Remember it's okay to use your imagination and your subconscious will work with you.

If your left hand was higher than the right, you may be resisting the suggestions more actively. You may want to reassess your fears or concerns about control. Reread my comments addressing the common fears about hypnosis starting on page 25 - 27. Having a reverse response also indicates you are susceptible to suggestion, but you need to control how it happens. The fact your hands did move is important. You can control the connection between your mind and your body and change the physical response.

Sometimes people hold their arms rigid because the feeling of the movement is a little scary or startling when it happens. If you are actively imagining and suddenly feel the arm move by itself, you may be surprised. The movement may be your first conscious awareness of a subconscious process. Remind yourself that it's okay, that you are developing a relationship to your subconscious. Can you remember the feeling of getting hungry? You can feel a very strong sensation in your stomach. This sensation is entirely controlled by a subconscious process. Since you're used to the feeling, you consider hunger normal. In self-hypnosis, you learn to cultivate subconscious responses. As with hunger, there will often be meaning to these movements. It can be a delightful experience when the subconscious 'guides' us in unexpected ways.

Here are some comments from students to this exercise:

"My left arm was stiff and my right arm was more fluid."

"I couldn't experience the balloon, but my left arm felt heavy."

"I was actually surprised. My left arm felt heavy and my right one light, but when I opened my eyes, they hadn't moved."

"I felt like I was fighting the up hand. When I started to imagine the balloon, I thought people would be watching me. I became self-conscious."

"I just put my left arm down, because I couldn't imagine myself holding a bucket for any length of time.

These comments illustrate how your mind may also be involved in whatever you are experiencing. This is okay. In self-hypnosis, you don't ever have to fight your mind. You will learn about yourself by paying attention to your responses to this exercise. Some senses may have been easier to imagine than others. Focus on these senses in your self-hypnosis practice. For example, I'm more of a kinesthetic, feeling person. I can feel the sensation of the balloon and the bucket easier than I can see them. I personally don't care what color the balloon is; the feeling is enough to draw me into trance. What senses are easier for you?

Did you notice other interesting sensations or changes? Anything you experienced during this exercise can be an indication of how you experience trance. Did you lose track of time? Did you feel a change in the temperature in your body? Did your awareness drift a little into a feeling or a thought? Did you forget about some part of your body, or some discomfort? These are all trance indicators, markers you can learn to recognize. Welcome these experiences when they occur and invite them into your next exercise. Were the feelings and responses you experienced familiar in some way? If so, you may have a familiarity with trance. Self-hypnosis can be one of the easiest things you learn to do, because you already know how.

The goal of this exercise isn't just getting the arms to move. You could easily move them consciously. Rather, the goal is to feel as if they begin moving by themselves. When your arms move, your subconscious will begin leading you into trance. Welcome all the sensations you experience, as part of the communication with your subconscious.

Any of the elements of this exercise can also become an induction to hypnosis; all you need to do is add intent. For example, as your arm gets heavier you could say to yourself, "As my arm gets heavier, I am becoming more relaxed." Your subconscious will respond to your suggestion. As you focus on the image of the bucket, you will have a response. Your arm will get heavier. Welcome and allow these changes and you will shift your orientation inwards and enter into trance.

If, at any time, stronger emotions surface during this or any other exercise, you can add an intention to soothe yourself. Make a conscious statement such as, "My experience of hypnosis is calming, comfortable and safe." There's no need to experience any discomfort with self-hypnosis. If you have strong emotional responses and you feel the need to do more work with them, then getting professional guidance can be extremely helpful. You can find a trained hypnotherapist or counselor in your area to help you do the work you need to do in an environment where you feel safe.

Now you have a better sense of the connection between your mind and your body. No matter what results you had, you may want to repeat this exercise -- you will learn more about yourself. In the next chapter, you will use this connection more intentionally in your first hypnotic induction.

mind and
body

Chapter 3
Beginning Practice

Abundance is not something we acquire. It is something we tune into.
Wayne Dyer

Exercise two - Heavy arm self-practice

Next, you will use part of the susceptibility test as an induction into self-hypnosis. You will use the image of the bucket with one of your arms. You will be leading yourself through the experience and with the intention to enter trance. By leading yourself, you will be responding to what is happening and using your experience as part of your induction. Set this guide in front of you so you can read it without straining. Then begin reading the script below.

Read the words slowly with intention. Let your voice relax. Pause at the end of each sentence and allow the words to settle in. As you read, enjoy the sound of the words as well as their meanings. Your subconscious will respond. Do what the words suggest. Pause regularly to allow the feelings you're experiencing to unfold. Find a comfortable upright position where you can breathe easily.

Heavy arm self-practice.
Materials needed - journal.
Time needed - 25 minutes.

Begin reading aloud softly to yourself:

Okay, (your name), take a nice deep breath in (breathe in) . . . and breathe out as you relax (breath out) . . . . You can continue breathing comfortably . . . and easily . . . throughout this experience. Any time you need to breathe while reading, you can pause and enjoy the flow of your breath.

Now, as you continue reading these words, I'd like you to raise up one of your arms and extend it either to the side of your body, or the front, with your palm facing down.

Now imagine an empty plastic bucket with a handle just beneath your hand.

Close your hand around the handle and hold on to it.

Notice the color of this bucket.

Enjoy imagining that color, though you may not see it with your physical eyes.

Now imagine there is a small stream of water pouring just past your fist and into the bucket.

Listen to the sound of the water landing inside the bucket.

Notice how the sound changes as the bucket starts to fill.

Enjoy the feeling of the weight as the bucket gets heavier.

You don't have to resist that feeling. In fact, as you feel the heaviness in the arm and the shoulder, your breath will continue relaxing.

Notice how the arm tends to rise a little when you breathe in . . . and lower when you exhale . . . . Allow this natural movement to take you deeper into relaxation.

Your arm may even begin moving slowly downwards if it hasn't already.

At some point, the arm will eventually touch down to the chair or your leg. When this happens all the muscles in your arm can let go and relax. Then your whole body can relax . . . and you can let go into a light, comfortable trance . . . even as you continue reading and speaking to yourself . . . .

Even now your body is already responding in just the right way for you.

When the arm touches down, your eyes can skip over to the words - Arm Down Now - printed in bold on the next page.

Now, (your name), notice where in your body you are feeling an interesting sensation . . . How would you describe that sensation? See what word or words come . . . and speak them aloud.

As you feel this (sensation), you are safe and comfortable and are learning how to experience a light trance. As this (sensation) becomes stronger, your arm will continue getting heavier, moving downwards all by itself.

As your arm goes deeper, you are also going comfortably, deeper into trance. As this happens, the bucket continues filling . . . the sound of the water continues . . . and the feeling of tiredness in the arm takes you deeper.

Breathing easily and naturally, you are learning to trust yourself more and more. Everything you are experiencing is happening in just the right way for you. You are remembering in a different way, that you are okay just the way you are.

Now, (your name), if your eyes finish reading this sentence before your arm touches down, let them drift back over to the sentence in bold that starts, "Even now your body . . . ", on the previous page and continue reading down from there.

Arm Down Now

Letting go now . . . feeling a wave of relaxation spread through your whole body. You've done very well (your name), allowing your body to help you into a light trance. When you read the words - eyes closing now - in bold below, you can let your eyes close comfortably and relax for one to three minutes, whatever length of time feels right for you. When your eyes are closed, you can let yourself drift into whatever feelings or sensations you enjoy. After the right amount of time, you can open your eyes and continue reading.

Eyes closing now.

Now, eyes open again . . . you can recreate any enjoyable feelings or sensations you are experiencing any time you practice self-hypnosis. You are already learning more about trance.

Now, (your name), in a moment I'm going to count up from One to Five. When I reach Five, you will return to your normal consciousness. You will remember what you've learned and experienced in this pleasant trance state.

Beginning, counting up to:

One. Starting to come gently out of trance.

Two. Becoming more aware and alert. Coming into your breathing. You are speaking a little louder.

Three. More aware and awake now, returning to normal. Beginning to move your fingers and toes.

Four. Almost there, almost completely back.

Five. All the way back to a full awareness.

Welcome back. Take a deep breath, stretch, and enjoy how you feel.

End reading aloud.

Personal responses

Well done! You have just gone through your first self-hypnosis experience. Now take a few moments while this experience is fresh in your mind and answer these questions:

1 - What are you feeling now?

2 - Did you experience anything interesting, surprising, or unusual during this exercise?

3 - What was your favorite or most interesting part of this exercise?

4 - Were there any difficult, frustrating, or uncomfortable parts of this exercise?

5 - Were any of your feelings or sensations familiar to you? Explain.

If you experienced any changes in your body, mind, or feelings during this exercise, then congratulate yourself. You successfully altered your awareness intentionally. Remember, self-hypnosis is a process of intentionally altering your awareness.

6 - How did your experience compare with your expectations of what trance should feel like? Was it what you expected, or different?

Discussion

Trance is not simply an "on" or "off" experience. There are many subtle gradations of depth and meaning. If you expected or wanted a more profound or altered experience, then be patient, you will have many opportunities to go deeper.

Self-hypnosis is a skill that takes practice. Whatever shifts you perceived with this first induction are valid trance experiences. By recognizing what happened, you validate your own unique experience. You will expand your sense of trance as you build your self-hypnosis practice. If you felt good and your body was relaxed afterwards, be glad. Self-hypnosis is inherently stress-reducing.

If you experienced other interesting or surprising sensations, take note of them. Unusual or unexpected experiences come directly from the subconscious. Like personal symbols in dreams, anything arising from your subconscious will carry personal meaning. The meaning may not be logical, but it brings forth energy and information from your deeper self. The more you do allow subconscious guidance in trance, the more profound and meaningful your experience of hypnosis will be. If a sensation you encounter feels awkward or a little scary, remind yourself, "This is a phenomena of trance. I'm okay. I am learning from my experiences."

Here are some comments from students regarding their trance experiences;

"It felt like coming home. I felt good."

"I had a sense in hypnosis that I could open my eyes and lift my arm if I wanted to. It was almost a reflex thought, like testing. I feel part of learning to allow and experience hypnosis is to also allow these thoughts and impulses to arise. They may even result in movement or physical resistance, but each time my resistance gets less strong as I become more comfortable with it. "

"If only for a few minutes, I felt a calmness. I believe I can return to that state."

Speaking or thinking to yourself, as you did with this last exercise, is one of the basic elements of self-hypnosis. You tell yourself what you want to do, then lead yourself into the experience. While in trance, you comment on what you are experiencing, add imagery, respond to arising thoughts and feelings, and allow whatever movements come from your subconscious. You will experience body sensations, thoughts, imagery, emotions, memories, and insights arising from within you. You can welcome everything you experience as part of your trance experience.

This last exercise was also more like true self-hypnosis since you started acknowledging the sensations you were having and using them as part of your induction. What was the interesting sensation you focused on during the exercise? By attending to it, and describing it, you validated what your subconscious provided. Then you added a conscious intention to it. This technique is called pacing and leading and is one of the most powerful components of self-hypnosis.

For example, in an induction, you may experience a wide range of changes: your vision may shift; your voice may get softer, or you may feel buzzing or tingling sensations in some part of your body. You may even feel an emotion arising from the subconscious. Some changes may be familiar; some are not. By allowing and pacing with the phenomena, you are saying to your subconscious, "Yes, I'm working with you on this one." Then, when you lead with a suggestion, your subconscious will also listen to you.

When you notice your breathing slowing down, add a thought, "As my breathing is slowing down, I'm going deeper into trance." Your suggestion leads you toward your goal.

Pacing and leading speeds up your induction into trance because you welcome whatever is happening. I'll say more about pacing and leading in chapter six. For now, remember; you don't have to resist anything in self-hypnosis. Self-hypnosis is a process that utilizes and validates everything you are experiencing. In the next chapter you will build on what you've started using the first person.

Chapter 4
Talking to Yourself

Self-suggestion makes you master of yourself.
W. Clement Stone

Exercise three - heavy arm, first person

The previous exercise was written in the second person. In trance this can be very effective. You are essentially telling the part of you having the experience what to do and what will happen. Next you will go through the same exercise in the first person. You can use your other arm if the first one is tired, or use the same arm if you want a stronger physical effect. This time, since you have a better idea what you will be doing, feel free to improvise. You can add other imagery or emphasize senses you enjoy. When you sense a shift in your awareness, comment on it (pacing), and tell yourself (leading), "As this is happening, I'm going deeper." Whenever your arm touches down, skip to that part of the induction.

Remember, getting the arm to drop quickly isn't the point of the procedure; allowing the experience to happen is. With practice, you can experience your arm operating independently of your conscious awareness. When it begins to drop down with heaviness, you welcome it as a movement arising from your subconscious. As the arm moves, add a suggestion, " . . . as I go deeper into trance," or " . . . becoming more relaxed." Your subconscious will take over to guide you deeper into trance.

Heavy arm self-practice - first person.
Materials needed - journal.
Time needed - 25 minutes.

Begin reading aloud and softly to yourself;
> Okay, now I can find a comfortable position, sitting upright, that allows me to breathe easily.
> Taking in a nice deep breath . . . and breathing out as I relax.
> I continue breathing comfortably . . . and easily throughout this experience. Any time I need to breathe while reading, I can pause and allow an easy breath.
> As I continue reading these words, I raise one of my arms and extend it horizontally out to the side of my body, palm facing down.
> Next I imagine an empty plastic bucket with a handle just beneath my hand.
> I close my hand around the handle and hold on to it.
> I allow any sense of color or sensation I have of this bucket.
> There is a small stream of water pouring into the bucket.
> I hear the splashing sound of the water.
> The sound changes as the bucket fills.
> I enjoy the sound changing as the bucket starts to fill.
> The bucket is getting heavier.
> I feel the sensation of weight get stronger as the bucket continues filling with water.
> As I feel the heaviness in my arm and shoulder, my breathing continues to relax.
> I notice how the arm tends to rise when I breathe in, and falls when I exhale.
> I allow this natural movement . . . and it takes me deeper into trance.
> My arm drops slowly and gently on its own as it gets heavier.
> When my arm touches down, all the muscles in the arm will let go and relax.
> Then, my whole body will relax, and I will experience a light comfortable trance.

Even now my body is already responding in just the right way for me.

> When the arm touches down, my eyes will skip over to the words - Arm Down Now - printed in bold on the next page.
> In my body I am feeling (name the sensation) .
> As I feel this (sensation), I know I am safe and comfortable and I am experiencing a light trance.
> As this (sensation) becomes stronger, my arm continues getting heavier, moving downwards all by itself.

With this (sensation), I am going deeper into trance.

As this happens, the bucket continues getting heavier . . . and the feeling of tiredness in the arm takes me deeper.

I am breathing easily and naturally and learning to trust myself more.

Everything I am experiencing is happening in just the right way for me.

I am remembering in a different way that I am okay just the way I am.

If my eyes finish reading this sentence before my arm touches down, they will drift over to the sentence in bold starting, "Even now my body is responding . . . ", on the previous page and continue reading down from there again.

Arm down now.

I let go now and feel a wave of relaxation spread through my entire body.

I've done very well allowing my body to help me into a light trance.

After I read the words - eyes closing now - in bold below, I will let the eyes close comfortably and relax for one to three minutes.

They will stay closed whatever length of time feels right for me.

When the eyes are closed, I will let myself drift into whatever feelings or sensations I enjoy.

When I'm ready, I will open the eyes and continue reading.

Eyes closing now

Now, the eyes are open again.

I am learning about trance.

I can enjoy the pleasant sensations I am experiencing any time I practice self-hypnosis.

In a moment I will count from One to Five. When I reach Five, I will return to normal consciousness.

I will remember what I've learned and experienced in hypnosis.

Beginning, counting up to:

One. Starting to come out of trance.

Two. Becoming more aware and alert . . . coming into my breathing. I'm speaking a little louder.

Three. More aware and awake now, returning to normal. Beginning to move my fingers and toes.

Four. Almost there, almost completely back.

Five. All the way back to normal consciousness.

End reading aloud.

Personal responses

Now take a few moments while this experience is fresh in your mind and answer these questions.

1 - What are you feeling now?

2 - What was different for you, doing this exercise the second time?

3 - Do you prefer using "I am . . . " or "You are . . . "?

4 - What familiar sensations or experiences might be indicators of trance for you?

5 - Any other thoughts or questions about your experiences this time?

Discussion

Now you have a sense of the different ways of speaking to yourself in trance. As you continue going through this workbook and practicing self-hypnosis, you may use which ever technique appeals to you. You can shift styles to emphasize different aspects of trance. For instance, you can say, "You are . . . " when you're feeling a little scattered and would like "someone else" who's more collected to guide you. When you want to emphasize and validate an important emotion, shift to, "I am strong and confident." Can you feel the difference in saying, "I am . . . " versus "You are . . ." with an emotion? Try it both ways for yourself.

Speak aloud:

"I am strong and confident."

Notice how these words make you feel.

Then, say,

"You are strong and confident."

Notice how these words make you feel.

You can switch between either style as you see fit.

Each time you do an exercise, you will get a better sense of how your awareness shifts when you go into trance. You may recognize you are in trance by any number of different phenomena occurring. Here's how some students describe their awareness of trance:

"I'm aware of my energy level and vibration. My hands are heavy. I'm often aware of daily things only when I come back out."

"I feel a sense of peace and varying levels of awareness."

"I have a feeling of depth."

"I recognize the feeling of heaviness, slowed respiration, and being focused and unfocused at the same time."

You might also sense a wide range of other phenomena: a slight change in the sensations in your body; a shift in the quality of your thinking; loss of sensation in a part of your body (analgesia); time slowing down, speeding up, or disappearing altogether; spontaneous memories or emotions appearing; things that aren't "really" there (positive hallucinations); a diminishing of pain (anesthesia); or simply feeling better. However you start to recognize your trance, pay attention to it. Then, use this awareness to lead yourself deeper using pacing and leading. Say, "As I feel this subtle shift, I am going deeper into trance."

If you sense something you're not quite comfortable with, suggest another kind of change. For instance, you hear a dog barking in the background and find it distracting, say, "As this sound drifts through my mind, I am letting go and relaxing." You can welcome the distraction as part of your process. You could also say, "And as I go deeper, the barking moves farther and farther away from me." It will move farther from your awareness.

Self-patter

In your self-talk during trance, you can develop simple, stock phrases that feel good and are easy to remember. Having simple, comfortable patter will engage your mind and allow you to let go easier. For instance, saying "deeper relaxed" in between other thoughts and feelings will reinforce your relaxation. Pause a moment, and say it softly to yourself now:

Deeper relaxed.

You can add those two words and enjoy how they make you feel when you don't really know what else to say. Another effective phrase is, "I'm okay." The more you say this to yourself, the more you will feel safer and more comfortable, regardless of what you are experiencing. You can develop a comfortable set of intentional, calming phrases. Say each of the following phrases to yourself and see how they feel. Rewrite the ones you like in your journal.

Breathing easy and naturally, going deeper relaxed.

With each feeling I experience . . . I'm okay.

So pleasantly heavy and calm.

Feeling soft and comfortable.

Drifting comfortably and tingling.

It's so easy to let go and relax.

Allowing everything as it's happening now.

So safe, comfortable and relaxed.

Drifting into this feeling, I'm more confident and calm.

It's so simple and easy.

Even now, there's nothing I need to do and nothing not to do.

Each thought, each sensation just drifting by on its own.

I am letting go now.

Noticing how easily I'm relaxing and letting go now.

Even this thought makes me go deeper.

Even this thought allows me to go deeper.

This feeling is spreading out through my whole body, so comfortable and safe.

That's great. I'm doing just fine the way I am. I'm okay.

Even as my mind wanders, I'm becoming more . . . (add your intent.)

You can use any of these phrases while you are practicing self-hypnosis. The regular use of these phrases will relax your mind, like the presence of a trusted friend. As you practice speaking to yourself, your patter phrases will become more natural and spontaneous. When your mind wants to engage in a thought, your familiar phrases will be there with you. In self-hypnosis, you don't ever have to fight the activity of your mind. Soothing words will arise and lead you right back into trance.

With any of the phrases above, you can add leading suggestions to point you toward your goal. The second half of each sentence below is the suggestion:

As this feeling is spreading out through my body, I'm going deeper into trance.

So safe, comfortable and relaxed and feeling more confident and in control.

So pleasantly heavy and calm now, everything is becoming easier.

Self patter is especially helpful if you enjoy more structure. Use familiar phrases if you enjoy having thoughts in your mind, rather than emptiness. Unlike some forms of meditation, where an empty mind is the goal, it doesn't matter in self-hypnosis if your mind is active. You can have thoughts in your mind while the rest of your being drops down into the experience of trance. When you allow the thoughts to be in your mind, you bring your mind into congruence with your overall intent. You can even comment on the thoughts objectively:

As these thoughts go through my mind, I am going deeper into trance.

As the mind is busy, I am calming and relaxing.

When you comment on your thoughts you dissociate from them and you associate with other, deeper levels of your being. During the last two arm drop inductions, there was also a shift in the way the arm was referenced. It started out being 'your arm' and then about half way through became 'the arm.' As you go into trance, you dissociate from the arm.

When you start to experience a body part or your thoughts behaving as if they had 'a mind of their own', you go deeper into trance. Dissociation tends to deepen trance because it allows your focus to turn more inward. Allowing "the arm" to do what it wants is a lot easier than trying to let "my arm" do something strange.

Anytime you sense something happening, acknowledge it as a thing, "out there", while you continue being "safe, comfortable and relaxed." You can let go of conscious control in a positive way. When you dissociate from things that have previously annoyed you, you will feel even more empowered and in control. For example, when the barking dog annoys you, comment on the feeling objectively, "My annoyance can rise and fall and I'm okay."

Since you've been guiding yourself for the last two exercises, this next one will be guided by me, with the CD. With a longer, guided induction, you can relax and go deeper into your experience of trance.

Chapter 5
Receiving Guidance

Go confidently in the direction of your dreams. Live the life you have imagined.
Henry David Thoreau

Exercise four - Longer guided induction

Again, for this exercise, find a comfortable position where you can be comfortable for 40 minutes, with your portable CD player. (This includes extra time to answer the questionnaire.) Loosen any restrictive clothing you are wearing; take off your glasses or contacts. Give yourself permission to enjoy this experience as deeply as you want. You can let go and immerse yourself in a comfortable, safe experience. As always, you can enter into your state of trance at your own pace. When finished, turn to page 59 and complete the response form.

Longer guided induction - CD exercise #2.
Materials needed - CD and portable player, journal.
Time needed - 40 minutes.

Preparation
To begin, find a comfortable position.

If at any time you need to move, you can do so.

You can always take care of yourself.

Now, you can relax . . . breathe comfortably . . . and listen to the sound of my voice.

Allow yourself to go along with and imagine what I say.

You don't need to force anything . . . you can let things happen as they occur.

I will act as a coach and guide so that you will be able to easily enter hypnosis yourself.

Induction - Eye-fixation

If you are lying down, I'd like you to focus your gaze at a spot on the ceiling. If you are sitting up, focus on a spot on the opposite wall.

It's okay if you're not wearing your glasses and your vision is blurry . . . just focus on a particular shape or color.

Pick a spot that forces the eyes to look up. You want to create a little tension in the muscles in your eyes.

Focus your gaze and your awareness on your chosen spot.

As you focus, allow your breathing to flow in and out easily and naturally.

You may find your eyes wander occasionally, but they can always return to your spot.

As you focus on the spot, all other thoughts and sensations arriving in your awareness will pass right through . . . like clouds drifting by on a sunny day.

And gradually, you will start to notice changes.

The muscles in and around your eyes may begin to feel a little tired.

Your vision may start to shift or change in some subtle way.

And your breathing may slow down more comfortably.

The longer you focus, the more things will start to change.

This is a natural process.

You can allow these changes as they happen.

The longer you focus, you will feel the muscles around your eyes becoming tired and heavy.

And you might imagine at some point, when the eyes seem to want to close all by themselves, they can do so.

And when they close, you can let go of any tension in your body and relax deeply.

Until then, enjoy and allow any sensations you experience, as the eyes become heavier and heavier.

So heavy . . . they will want to blink if they haven't already.

They can blink as much as they like.

Letting everything happen . . . just as it wants to happen.

You might even imagine little weights gently pulling down on the eyelids.

If the eyes close and I'm still talking about the eyes, you can just drift deeper, enjoying your inner sensations.

So . . . the longer you focus, the more heavy the eyes become.

As you let everything please itself, even letting those blinks become slower and bigger, the eyelids getting very, very heavy and tired . . . they will want to close.

When they do, you will go down deeply . . . into a pleasantly relaxed state.

Until then notice and enjoy how heavy and tired the eyes become, how each blink seems to get heavier and slower all by itself, pulling you down into a more comfortable, relaxed state.

When the eyes decide it's right, they will close all by themselves, closing down firmly and comfortably, taking you down with them . . . deeper and deeper.

Letting go is so easy and comfortable. It's so easy to let your experience happen all by itself.

You are drifting further and further away on the sound of my voice.

It is really so very simple and easy . . . . not needing to do anything . . . or trying not to do anything.

You are feeling very good in every way, feeling safe and secure and comfortable.

The deeper you go, the better you feel, and the better you feel, the deeper you go.

And now, becoming more relaxed, it doesn't even matter any more what the eyes are doing, closed or open . . . no matter. They will close when they're ready, if they're not already closed.

Take a deep relaxing breath . . . and exhale any remaining tension you feel in your head and face.

The body can move if it needs to, without disturbing this deeply relaxed feeling, this felt sense of well-being.

As deep as you go, you can always hear the sound of my voice.

Deepening - Counting with body relaxation

In a few moments I'm going to begin counting slowly backwards, from ten down to one.

As I count, you will feel your body relaxing more and more, as you feel yourself drifting comfortably into a deeper and deeper state of trance.

As each number drifts by, let another part of your mind repeat the number to yourself, like an echo . . . an echo.

As you hear the numbers echoing in your mind, you will relax even more.

You may also see the number drift through your inner vision, taking you into a more comfortable place.

The deeper you go, the more comfortable and safe you become.

Until at the count of one you will be deeply relaxed and in a pleasant, comfortable hypnotic state.

So, beginning with . . .

Ten - seeing the number, and hearing an echo inside, allowing all the muscles in your face to loosen up and relax.

Relaxation spreads through your eyes, your nose and mouth . . . and your jaw.

Nine - a relaxing calmness eases down through all the muscles in your neck.

Eight - and down into all the muscles and nerves in your shoulders.

You are more and more relaxed, deeper and deeper.

Seven - down, relaxation drifting down through your chest and upper back, deeply and comfortably.

Six, echoing softly inside and letting the relaxation spread to your upper arms.

Five - flowing down into your forearms, into your hands and all the way out the tips of your fingers.

Four - relaxation flowing down through the center of your body, into your abdomen and lower back, deeper and calmer.

Three - letting the relaxation spread down through your pelvis and your groin, front and back, flowing down into your legs, and knees.

Two - flowing down through your lower legs, all the way down to your feet and the tips of your toes.

One - all the way down, much deeper, letting your whole body relax deeply, melting away any remaining tension and smoothing out, deeper and completely relaxed.

That's good! As deep as you go, always feeling just right inside, more and more comfortable, safe and relaxed.

Now, you can drift in between the words I say, not even needing to pay attention to each individual word . . . enjoying your own sense of relaxation, your own felt sense of well-being.

There is absolutely nothing you need to do, just allow your own felt sense to unfold.

Deepening - pleasant place and senses

And as you drift now, you may remember a very pleasant place, some place where you felt just right - comfortable, calm, and alive.

This place may be real or imaginary, inside or out, just what feels right for you.

Engage your senses in this safe place and go deeper into trance.

You may also remember an image that captivated you - a sunset, a mountain view, or an image that seemed to draw you out of yourself.

Enjoy your image, and the colors, the shapes and the feelings that awaken in you.

In this place you might recall a piece of fruit you particularly enjoyed, remembering the taste and the smell . . . all the sensation of it, and the feeling of nourishment flowing into your body.

You may even remember a captivating sound . . . it might be a certain music . . . or a natural sound.

Enjoy the sound as it soothes your whole being.

You can let yourself drift into and through all these sensations, going deeper, becoming more comfortable and more relaxed.

I'm okay

Now, from within your experience, find a word that describes what you are feeling. Allow the right word to come to mind.

Say to yourself, "I am feeling (your word)." Validate yourself.

Now, this time, say to yourself, "I am feeling (your word)" and add "and I'm okay just the way I am."

"I am feeling (your word) and I'm okay just the way I am."

Say the whole sentence to yourself, either aloud or in your mind.

Say it again, softly to yourself, and feel the words down through your whole body.

With this phrase, you validate yourself. You are okay right now, just the way you are.

You can recognize what you are feeling at any time of your day, and add the thought, "and I'm okay."

You will empower yourself each time you do so.

Suggestions

As the following words drift by, your subconscious will attend to the ones that truly resonate with you.

Each time you experience this felt sense of well-being, it becomes more natural for you.

You can access your own inner wisdom and intelligence, again . . . easier and easier . . . each time you enter this state of self-hypnosis.

You are learning now . . . understanding . . . knowing your own felt sense of trance.

You are empowered . . . stronger . . . clearer in your mind and body.

This feeling now, connects with other times . . . other memories . . . when you felt so good and strong . . . so comfortable, and alive.

You can return here . . . again and again . . . easier and easier . . . into trance, whenever you desire.

As you come to know hypnosis and trance, your own practice will become a natural, effortless part of you.

As you now understand how simple and effective self-hypnosis is, you will find the time to practice at home, or at work . . . or anywhere that feels just right.

Each time you experience hypnosis, you will allow just the right amount of time to learn more, to deepen the connection to yourself.

You may enjoy a few moments of learning relaxation . . . an easy remembering of new thoughts and ideas.

Or a longer time, and a deeper learning.

It may be in the morning . . . at a break in the middle of the day . . . or at night.

You are now taking charge of your life. Feeling calm and relaxed, but also clear and strong, healthy and alive . . . learning from experiencing . . . learning from inside your own feeling.

Even now, deeper relaxed.

Awakening

From where ever you are now . . . in a few moments, I'm going to count up from One to Five. When I reach Five, you will be awake, alert, refreshed, and feeling good all over.

You will remember everything you've experienced that you want to remember.

You'll find you can sleep very deeply and profoundly tonight and awaken refreshed in the morning.

You'll find you'll have very vivid, colorful, and pleasant dreams you can remember.

The next time you want to experience hypnosis you will be able to go into a comfortable trance faster and easier, because you are becoming familiar with hypnosis now.

You can only be hypnotized when you want to and in a way that serves you.

All right . . . beginning to come back . . . coming up a little ways to One.

Feelings starting to come back into your body, coming up a little more to Two, coming back into your breath.

Beginning to sense your body and coming up a little more to Three . . . beginning to move a little, fingers . . . toes . . . breathing.

All the feelings starting to come back, coming up a little more to Four.

Getting ready to come all the way back, coming all the way up to Five.

That's good. Stretch. Take a deep breath, and open your eyes.

Stop the CD and fill out the questionnaire in the workbook.

End induction.

Personal responses

Take a few moments now, as this experience is fresh in your mind, and answer these questions:

1 - What are you feeling right now? Write the phrase, "I am feeling . . . " and add your word.

2 - Did you experience anything interesting, surprising, or unusual during this exercise?

3 - What was your favorite or most interesting part of this exercise?

4 - Were there any difficult, frustrating, or uncomfortable parts in this exercise?

5 - Any other thoughts about the experiences you had?

Now I would like you to consider each of the following parts to this induction. Attending to each part will help you get a better sense of which techniques work well for you and which ones don't. If there are parts you don't remember, that's okay. You may have been drifting deeper for a time. You can listen to the exercise again to get the parts you missed.

6 - Listening to voice and being guided. During this exercise you were guided by listening to a voice. Did you enjoy being guided, or find yourself wanting to go into other sensations or places? If so, note what you liked or disliked and what you prefer.

7 - Eye-fixation. This exercise began when you focused on a spot. Then came heaviness in the eyes, other perceptual changes, and eventually eye-closure and relaxation. Did you enjoy the eye fixation induction or find it difficult? Was it helpful for you?

8 - Counting down with body relaxation. The deepening used numbers while relaxing your way down through the body to deepen your trance. Did you enjoy counting with relaxation or find it difficult? Was it helpful for you?

9 - Pleasant place and senses. Your second deepening used imagining and sensing a pleasant place with enjoyable senses from your memory. Did you enjoy this part or find it difficult? Was it helpful for you?

10 - I'm okay. You allowed a word to come to mind, describing what you were feeling. Then you added the words, "I'm okay." You spoke the phrase, "I am feeling (your word) and I'm okay" to yourself. Did you enjoy this part or find it difficult? Was it helpful for you?

11 - Suggestions. In trance, you heard suggestions about: learning trance, hypnosis becoming natural and effortless, increasing understanding, and forming a self-hypnosis practice. Did you enjoy this part or find it difficult? Was it helpful for you?

12 - Awakening. In your awakening you received reminders of how you are in control, can sleep well and dream, can remember what you want, and can experience hypnosis when you want to. Then you were counted up from 1 to 5, returning to an awake, normal state. Did you enjoy this part or find it difficult? Was it helpful for you?

Discussion

The guided induction you just experienced is an example of the complete structure you will be using in your self-hypnosis practice. This exercise included an induction (eye-fixation), two deepenings (counting while relaxing and imagining senses), suggestions, and an awakening. Each of the parts blend and flow into the other, but each also occurs in a specific order. What you start with is the induction, what you use to "go deeper" is the deepening. There are many, many different inductions and deepenings, so if the ones used in this exercise were awkward or uncomfortable for you in any way, don't worry about it. You will find techniques that work well for you.

Take special note of which parts you liked in this last exercise. Take a moment and read over the script of that part. Enjoy the experience again as you read it. This way you can begin integrating the parts you like into your own process. Each time you read a script you will learn to allow your own trancing more easily. Also, pay attention to any shifts or changes you experience in your body, mind, or emotions during each exercise. Changes coming from your subconscious are indicators of your experience of trance. Here are some comments from students regarding their experiences of the guided induction;

"I was relaxing, focusing my eyes, then counting down. Then I must have drifted off. The next thing I remember is counting up and it being over."

"I know when I was in it. I was somewhere, but now I'm not so sure."

"I felt a tingle go down my arms."

"My eyes started to get heavy before you suggested it. I felt it happening all by itself."

"When I was relaxing my body, I drifted and remembered my father. I was a real little girl and he was swinging me between his legs. I must have been really little. I felt safe and loved. I hadn't thought about him for a long time."

Drifting, feeling something you can't quite describe, feeling a physical sensation happening all by itself, and remembering an event or an emotion spontaneously are all indicators of trance. What was your trance experience?

Your first exercises started with the arm drop and eye-fixation techniques for a specific reason -- they both use the physical body. Using an induction involving the physical body is especially effective because you don't have to rely entirely on the mental process. When you're stressed or anxious you might have a hard time focusing your mind on an inward image or feeling. In these situations, having something physical and tangible to focus on is easier. Physical inductions quickly lead you back into inner processes, feelings and imagery. Starting with the physical, they make it easier to shift from a stressed or tense feeling to a more comfortable one.

If you are familiar with relaxation techniques, you may have found the physical techniques a little tedious. You might have wanted to go inwards and relax sooner. If so, then I advise you to do the physical inductions. They provide a different perspective on tension. Creating some tension and holding it, allows you to relax deeper when you let go. As you become more familiar with the experience of self-hypnosis, you can go directly into trance when you're ready, skipping the overt, physical inductions. If you ever need a more tangible beginning, you can use the eye-fixation or arm drop inductions. You will work more with tension in the progressive relaxation technique in Chapter 10.

If you experienced any frustrations or difficulties with this longer induction, be sure to attend to them. You may need to change something to better suit you. For instance, your body may have bothered you in some way. When this happens, check to see if there's something you can do to make yourself more comfortable. Do you need to move your body or adjust your position? Remember, you can also move your body while you're experiencing hypnosis. You may not want to move in trance, feeling it will disturb your experience, but moving will help you go deeper as you'll be more comfortable.

Any unaddressed fears or beliefs can also disrupt your experience. For instance, if your body keeps fidgeting, your subconscious may be telling you it does not want to relax. A deeper part of you might not feel safe. If there is no physical reason for your discomfort, then take another look at your fears. What would be the worst thing that could happen if you did relax and experience a trance? Ask yourself and see what answer comes. Addressing your fears will help you to let them go. Then read more about trance and soothe yourself with the knowledge that trance is safe. You can experience self-hypnosis in just the right way for you. (Feel free to reread the earlier sections on fears and beliefs in chapter one.)

You may also have expectations about what kind of experience you're supposed to have. These expectations can get in the way. For instance, you may think you need an absolutely quiet space to do self-hypnosis. If there is noise, it may irritate you and disrupt your experience. You may also be irritated by body sensations or a busy mind. One way to respond to these distractions is to let go of your expectations and welcome what is happening as part of your process. You can say to yourself, "As my mind is busy, I'm still able to experience hypnosis," or "As I hear the dog barking, the sound passes through me. I am relaxing more." You can experience hypnosis in any environment. Athletes go into trance during extreme physical events and with crowd noise. Even people with chronic pain can experience a profound state of trance. You can experience trance when you let go of your expectations and allow the experience you are having. It takes practice to utilize everything that is happening.

If you fell asleep during this induction, you may have missed significant parts. This is okay. Your subconscious will still attend to what is being said, though your conscious mind may not be as satisfied. Often people are surprised how they awaken when the numbers are counting up from One to Five. Some part is listening. If you missed some part of this exercise, then sit upright when you listen to the induction, or do it in the morning when you're more refreshed.

Falling asleep may also indicate you need rest. Most of us live very busy lives. Any quiet moments we experience tend to lead to a sleeping state. Make sure you get the sleep you need. Sleep is one of the best cures for stress and tension. Also, self-hypnosis is a particular state of being where the body is very relaxed, as it is in sleep, yet the mind is still alert. Learning to enter this state, you may sometimes miss the mark, and go too deep. With practice you will be able to relax your body very deeply and still be mentally aware. This is the ideal state for working with trance.

This exercise added a very basic, powerful affirmation, "I'm okay." How did it feel to you to add the words, "I'm okay" to a feeling you were experiencing? Using these words will remind you at a deep level that you are okay, regardless what you are experiencing. Saying, "I'm feeling (your word) and I'm okay" allows you to feel emotions safely. You can use this phrase to soothe yourself any time of day, in or out of trance. The simplest way is to pause a moment, take a deep breath in, then exhale, relax, and say, "I'm okay." You will feel a settling of your emotional body. If you want the affirmation to be more effective, start by checking into what you are feeling and put a word to it. Be honest with yourself. Then say the whole phrase, "I am feeling (your word) and I'm okay." When you're in an emotion, you are in trance and open to suggestion. Your subconscious will attend to your suggestion and make it happen. You will experience a shift, even if your conscious mind doesn't believe you're okay.

After the induction ended, the first question was, "What are you feeling?" Even then you can put that feeling into an "I am feeling . . . " phrase. Each time you recognize and speak your feelings, you validate yourself. Coming out of trance, you may be feeling a wide range of responses. They're all okay. They're all part of your learning. Here are some examples from students coming out of trance:

I am confused.

I am focused.

I am calm.

I am frustrated.

I am at peace.

I am excited.

In any class, the responses are always varied. Your feelings are unique. Understand that whatever you are feeling, you can respond to it and take care of yourself. What if you felt confused or uncomfortable at the end of the induction? What would you need to do to take care of yourself? Initially, you could simply add, "and I'm okay" to your statement. Say the whole thing to soothe yourself. "I'm feeling frustrated and I'm okay." Then you could take steps to address your frustration. What caused it? Explore your feelings. You may have had an unexpected or disorienting experience. Wherever you are, you can address your need to understand and know what your feelings are about. Each time you attend to your feelings and respond consciously, you learn how to take care of yourself and how to empower yourself.

With this last exercise, you had the opportunity to go deeper with a guided induction. Next we'll further explore how the induction process works and how pacing and leading makes your trance practice more effective.

deeper

relaxed

Chapter 6
Leading Yourself

The real distinction is between those who adapt their purposes to reality and those who seek to mold reality in the light of their purposes.
Henry Kissinger

More about inductions

Eye-fixation was the induction for this last exercise. Whenever you focus your eyes on something and hold that focus, they will tire. Adding a suggestion that something else will happen when the eyes get tired and close is what makes this natural process an induction. The rest of your body relaxing isn't necessarily associated with eye fatigue. When you add the suggestion, you are telling your subconscious what you want to happen. Then, when the feelings start to occur in your eyes, your subconscious also accepts the idea. Once you state your intent, all you have to do is allow and enjoy what naturally happens in your eyes; the subconscious provides the rest. It's that simple.

These are the basic elements of all hypnotic inductions and deepenings: you set up a specific event -- something that will happen -- then you tell yourself what will happen when the event occurs. You then let go and allow the subconscious to make it happen.

Here are some examples of how you might already induce every day trances:

You say, "When I get home, I'll finally be able to relax." Then you enjoy your drive home and when you get there, you feel relaxed.

You say, "When I finish this class, I'll feel confident about computers." Then you enjoy your class and finish feeling confident.

You say, "When I get to the city, I'll feel stressed." Then you allow your arrival into the city to distress you.

You say, "When I get back to my neighborhood, I'll know I'm safe." Then you drive home and as you see familiar landmarks, you start to relax and feel safe.

You say, "I feel self-conscious when I speak in front of people." Then, as you start thinking about speaking in front of people, you start worrying. When you finally get in front of the group, you feel self-conscious and nervous.

The connections we make between events and feelings lead us into specific experiences. Some we enjoy; some make us uncomfortable. These "truths" may be based on past experiences we've had. You may know that when you get home you relax. It's logical. Your home is safe, comfortable and familiar. Though this conclusion is logical, when you think suggestive thoughts to yourself, you're also leading yourself into the next experience, whether or not outside events have anything to do with it. Physically, you will feel safer as soon as you get back to your home just because you've created an expectancy. The feeling occurs as soon as you see the familiar buildings and streets. In the same way, you may start to get self-conscious as you approach a public speaking event.

In self-hypnosis, you create expectancy consciously. You decide what you want to experience and you tell yourself when it will happen. Self-suggestion is a tremendously powerful tool for transforming the way you experience your interaction with the world. As you learn about inductions and the experience of hypnosis, you will become more aware of other ways you are inducing certain states. Some serve you and some are old, habitual programs. You can recognize these old patterns and reassess their value to you. You can change yourself.

So here are some examples of how suggestion is used in hypnosis;

When my breathing slows down, I will feel better.
When the eyes get heavy, I will let go and become more comfortable.
When I reach the number one, I will be in a deep state of hypnosis.
Each time I practice hypnosis, I become more confident.

What's so delightful about this process is that you don't have to consciously know how you are going to achieve a specific goal. Consider the idea of "becoming healthier." How do you do create health? Consciously, you may have no idea, but subconsciously the body, the heart, and the deeper mind all know what "healthier" means. Your subconscious makes it happen in the same way you physically become more comfortable when you walk into your home or sit in your favorite chair.

What's even more interesting is that the connection you make between the event and the result doesn't have to be logical. For instance, you might say to yourself, "When my arm raises up, I will be much more relaxed." This is what happens in an arm levitation induction. It's not logical that you would end up more relaxed since it takes more muscular energy for the arm to lift. But it works! Incidentally, arm levitation works especially well if you have lots of physical energy or nervousness to begin with. You will get a chance to practice the arm levitation induction in chapter 15.

With every induction you do, remember to add an intention. Tell yourself what you want to occur and when. It can be very simple, e.g., "When the eyes close, I will relax into a safe, comfortable trance experience."

Pacing and leading

The process of pacing and leading is similar to inductions, except you pace with what is currently happening and lead to what you want to have happen.

As the eyes are blinking, I am going into trance.
As I feel this warmth in my body, I am becoming more confident.
As my mind is distracted, I am going into trance.
As my breathing slows down, I have more and more energy.

The reason why pacing and leading work, and for that matter, why they are effective, is because this technique bridges the conscious and subconscious intentions. You are validating and utilizing what the subconscious is already presenting you. You don't consciously blink your eyes, warm your body, have a distracted mind, or slow down your breathing; these are all handled by the subconscious. By pacing with what you are experiencing, you validate the subconscious. The subconscious responds, "Yes, thank you," and becomes receptive. Then the subconscious will accept whatever conscious intention you add as a literal truth. The subconscious operates under a different kind of logic. It uses a different language of metaphor, symbols, feelings, and meaning. To the subconscious, it doesn't have to make sense of how an arm raising relates to relaxation or how a feeling of warmth in the body leads to an emotional feeling of confidence. The subconscious simply responds to the idea by making it so.

You may think it strange the way I'm talking about the subconscious as if it had intention and feelings, as though it really would respond to recognition. Consider this: the subconscious is a much larger reflection of conscious awareness. If you treat your subconscious as an equal part of the larger being that you are, you will live much more to your full potential.

You may have to practice validating your subconscious. After all, you have been taught to control the body, which is one of the largest channels of communication to the subconscious. You also may have been taught that your imagination has no value and your subconscious is to be feared. This conditioning puts you out of touch with the natural intelligence within you. As you learn the practice of pacing and leading, you will cultivate a more healthy relationship with your subconscious. Here's how one student described her experience:

> "I've gone into trance my whole life, but not with intent. It's a whole different experience acknowledging my subconscious. It's like there's a part of me saying, 'I'm so glad you finally found me. You're paying attention to me.' I have a feeling of two parts working together."

So, when you're going into trance and something arises in your body, like a twitch or a movement, allow it. Let it happen as part of your conscious intention. The subconscious is working with you, but in its own way. You can welcome its movements as part of your self-hypnosis process, even if they seem at odds with your conscious focus. Pace with what you are experiencing and continue leading yourself toward your goal. The more honestly you speak to and acknowledge the subconscious forces within you, the more effective your pacing and leading will be. When you're feeling an awkward or uncomfortable emotion, speak to it. Validate it. Be honest with yourself. For example, you might say to yourself, "As I'm feeling confused and uncomfortable, I am learning about hypnosis. I am becoming a better person."

Pacing and leading are most effective when you pace with what you actually are experiencing, not what you want or expect to happen. Suppose you are sitting down to do self-hypnosis and you're feeling irritated, distracted and have a sore back. You could say to yourself, "As I'm doing self-hypnosis, I'm becoming more relaxed," which may be partially true. You will get much better results though, if you start with what you are actually experiencing, e.g., "As I feel this irritation and distraction, I am becoming more relaxed." To do pacing and leading effectively, you have to consciously recognize what is happening. You also have to know your goals. You'll work on this next in chapter 7 as you develop your own personalized auto-suggestion.

Chapter 7
Words That Empower You

The soul answers never by words,
but by the thing itself that is inquired after.
Ralph Waldo Emerson

Create your auto-suggestion

In hypnosis, you become more receptive to ideas you encounter. Your subconscious responds to suggestions. In trance you don't do everything suggested, rather, you follow ideas that resonate with you. If someone suggested you cluck like a chicken and behave in a way that didn't serve your intentions, you simply wouldn't do it. You wouldn't have to explain to yourself why; you would know what was right or wrong for you. Favorable ideas, however, are accepted at a very deep level. Suggestion is one of the most powerful aspects of hypnosis. Working with suggestions allows you to create the best inner environment to manifest your intentions.

Do you remember the suggestions I gave you during the last induction? They had to do with learning hypnosis, feeling safe and finding time to practice. How did they feel to you? Were there some that felt particularly good? Were there some you felt like ignoring? There's a good chance some of the words I spoke fit with your intentions. If you pay attention, you will feel a difference when a particular phrase resonates with you.

Your subconscious does respond with a feeling of "Yes!" when you encounter a particularly relevant idea. Your next step in learning self-hypnosis will be to create auto-suggestions ideally suited to your goals and needs. You want every idea you bring to mind in trance to be tailored to meet your personal needs, so you can bring a conscious and enthusiastic "Yes!" to it.

I will guide you through the process of writing an effective auto-suggestion. You will think about what you want to accomplish and you will clarify your specific goals and intentions. The work you do on your auto-suggestion is important and worth the effort. Writing down and clarifying your intentions engages your conscious mind with your intent. You send a message to your subconscious that you are serious. When you take change seriously, your subconscious listens. When you go into trance, the work you've done clarifying your conscious intent will pay off. The more clear and concise your suggestions are, the more effective they are in trance. In hypnosis, your conscious focus and intent works with your subconscious.

Creating your own auto-suggestion.
Materials needed - journal.
Time - variable, at least one hour.

To begin, I'd like you to revisit this question:

Why do you want to learn self-hypnosis? Write down your thoughts now.

Your intention can simply be to better yourself or to learn the process of hypnosis. Your entire self-hypnosis practice will help you with these goals. I want to suggest, however, you can also create very specific, tangible changes in your life. You manifest specific goals through cultivating clear intention and writing your auto-suggestion. There are virtually an unlimited number of things you can change or improve in yourself with self-hypnosis. For example, you might want to lose weight, gain self-esteem, gain self-confidence and self-trust, improve learning, overcome a fear, learn a new skill, learn a new way of handling an emotion, relieve anxiety, quit smoking, change a bad habit, instill a new habit, improve sleep, improve or enhance sexuality, improve creativity, improve performance, become more emotionally stable or become more emotionally expressive.

Write down a list of the things you would like to change or create in yourself. Put down anything that comes to mind.

Now prioritize your list. Go through and number each item from the most important to the least. What would be the first, most important thing, you want to change in your life? Rewrite your list with the ten most important things, the most important one leading the list. Here is an example list:

1   gain self-confidence
2   stop being angry
3   get a new job
4   etc.

The first item on your list will become your focus for self-hypnosis. If you've already been thinking about change, then picking a primary focus is fairly easy. You may also have several different, equally important topics. Some of the items on your list may seem different, but may actually be related in some way. For example, a woman in one of my classes wanted to quit smoking. As she thought about the times she had quit, she realized she had also felt more confident during those times. She decided self-confidence might be a better goal. As she weighed her options, she realized her need to quit smoking was stronger. Smoking had a more direct, negative impact on her life. So, she made quitting smoking her primary focus and added some suggestions for self-confidence. For someone else who was an infrequent smoker, not noticing much negative impact, the decision may have been reversed.

When you pick your focus, choose goals that are more "do-able." You may want a Ph.D., but that may be four or six years away, whereas "improving study skills" may be a much more practical goal to achieve your immediate needs. If you focus on your study skills, you can also include a few words directed to your Ph.D. "Being more comfortable in public" might be the more immediate goal than "being a good public speaker."

Also, don't underestimate yourself. If you're ready for change, go for the most important goal. Think about each goal you want to achieve. Be aware which one activates you. Remember, you can start simple and build up to more challenging goals as you learn to use your self-hypnosis skills.

Now, write down one goal you are going to focus on. Remember, if it's really not the right one you can always change it. To get started, though, you need some focus.

Write in your journal: With self-hypnosis I am going to (your goal).

To build an effective auto-suggestion, you're going to need specifics. To do this, start thinking about actually achieving this goal. What will happen when you have achieved this goal? How will your life be different? How will you feel, think and act? As you think about these things, write whatever comes to mind. Here's an example:

"My goal for self-hypnosis is to lose weight."

"I'm going to lose weight. My waist size will be smaller and I'll be able to fit into my favorite jeans. I'm not going to eat junk food. I can feel better and enjoy my body more. I will be happier and more confident. I'm going to enjoy exercising more. My body will be more toned and I will look better. I will be attractive and feel sexy. I can eat better. I won't snack when I'm not really hungry. I will drink lots of fluids. I won't snack on sugar and chips. I will stop eating when I'm not hungry. I don't have to eat all the food on my plate. I will find time to exercise. I will feel better about myself and I'll be able to make other changes in my life. Etc."

As you elaborate on your goal, put down everything that comes to mind. Don't edit or filter your writing. Try to include specific examples of how your life will change. Will your relationships with others be different? What other far-reaching effects will you experience? Let yourself write freely, whatever comes to mind. Don't hold back.

Elaborate on your goal now. Take your time (15 minutes is a good length of time).

Now you will revise what you've written, shaping your thoughts and ideas into an effective auto-suggestion. Following are the guidelines to refine your thoughts. With each guideline, I've included examples from the goal I used above. Read through these guidelines first; then you'll have an opportunity to use them to revise your suggestions.

1 - Be positive.

Instead of saying "I won't snack on sugar and chips," you could change this to, "I eat only healthy foods." Or, "When I snack, I eat only when I'm hungry and I eat healthy foods."

Don't use, "I can't . . . ", "I won't . . . ", or "Not this . . . "

Do use, "I am . . . " and "I can . . . "

2 - Present tense-present progressive, use "I am . . . ." or "I am becoming . . . "

Instead of saying, "I will be . . . " or "I am going to . . . ", you can say, "I am becoming lighter", "I am eating healthy", and "I feel so good as I am becoming healthier."

This guideline addresses how your subconscious will respond literally. If you say "I will" it means not now, but later. Shifting to "I am" makes it present. When you hear "I am" in trance, you will feel what you're talking about as if it's happening. You can even say "I am" to something you haven't experienced yet. Your subconscious will respond.

If using the present tense is too much of a stretch, then use what feels right. Saying, "I am 25 pounds lighter," may not fit when you haven't lost those pounds. Instead, say it as positively as feels right for you, e.g., "I am feeling lighter and my body is changing." The feeling can be present tense. "I will soon be 25 pounds lighter." The physical is soon to come!

3 - Affirm action, not ability, not "I can . . . ", but "I do" or "I am."

Instead of saying, "I can exercise more . . . ", I say, "I am exercising more," and "I am eating healthy foods."

4 - Be detailed. Think it through and be specific.

"I want to eat better" becomes "I am eating more grains and green vegetables. I am eating the right amount of food. I am taking my time eating the food I enjoy." "I am drinking lots of fluids" becomes "I am drinking four glasses of juice and spring water each day."

5 - Use your own words and language.

As you rewrite, make sure to use words and phrases that fit you. If you read other suggestions and like what they say, be sure they fit you. Also, instead of having long complex sentences, break them up into short, specific statements, e.g., "I am eating better. I am feeling better. I enjoy my body."

6 - Be realistic with numbers, amounts and actual activity.

"I am exercising three times a week. I will soon be 25 pounds lighter. I will fit into size 32 waist."

7 - Exaggerate and emotionalize feelings, senses, and the results of actions.

This is one of the most important guidelines for writing suggestions. You can't overdo the feelings and emotions you will experience when you change. Instead of, "I will feel better," elaborate on it, "I am feeling really great, excited, full of joy and vitality." Follow other statements you make with the resulting feelings. For example, "As I choose healthy foods, I feel great. When I recognize I'm full and stop eating, I feel strong, confident and empowered."

8 - Time limit for suggestion: When will it be?

If you have a time limit for any of your goals, be sure to include it. For example, "I will fit comfortably into my favorite jeans by my birthday." It's important to pick a realistic goal, one that feels right and attainable.

9 - Repetition can be good: Reemphasize key concepts.

"I am feeling lighter and happier." Repeat this several times.

10 - Establish key words, a key phrase or a symbol capturing the essence of your intentions.

The sample I've been using, "I am lighter and happier," would make a good key phrase. If, for example, I had a feeling of movement and energy with my weight loss, I could also use the phrase, "dancing in light," to capture the feeling of the changes I'm making. If you are a visual or a symbolic thinker then let your creativity lead you. What's important is that this key phrase connects you to your intent. Does your key phrase evoke the essence of your intent? Add your key phrase at the beginning, middle, and end of your suggestion.

11 - Include details on how achieving your goal will actually affect your life.

If you're focusing on self-confidence, joyfulness, or being happier, then your suggestion may be focused mostly on inner feelings. Add the physical manifestations of these changes. How will self-confidence change the way you act at work? "I enjoy talking with my co-workers." "As I feel joy, I dance more often." How will feeling confident manifest in your relationships? "As I am more confident, I stand up for myself at work. I look my co-workers in the eye when I talk with them. I feel strong and in control when I talk to my family. I am standing straighter and taller when I walk through my work place."

When you incorporate these eleven guidelines, your auto-suggestion will be very effective. The next step for you is to read through what you've written so far. For each sentence you have, you will add to it, clarify, or change it using each of the guidelines. I'll show you an example of rewriting. Each example is altered a bit using each guideline. I would start with my first draft on confidence:

"I'm going to lose weight. My waist size will be smaller and I'll be able to fit into my favorite jeans. I'm not going to eat junk food. I can feel better and enjoy my body more. I will be happier and more confident. I'm going to enjoy exercising more. My body will be more toned and I will look better. I will be attractive and feel sexy. I can eat better. I won't snack when I'm not really hungry. I will drink lots of fluids. I won't snack on sugar and chips. etc . . . "

Using guideline #1, Be positive, I would make these changes:

"I'm going to lose weight. My waist size will be smaller and I'll be able to fit into my favorite jeans. I am going to eat healthy foods. I feel better and enjoy my body more. I will be happier and more confident. I'm going to enjoy exercising more. My body will be more toned and I will look better. I will be attractive and feel sexy. I can eat better. I will eat only when I'm hungry. I will drink lots of fluids. When I eat, I will choose healthy foods. etc . . . "

Then I'd go through the everything I'd written again using guideline #2 - Present tense-present progressive, use "I am . . . ." or "I am becoming . . . " I would make these changes;

"I'm going to lose weight. My waist size is becoming smaller . I will soon be able to fit into my favorite jeans. I am eating healthy foods. I can feel better and enjoy my body more. I am becoming happier and more confident. I am enjoying exercising more. My body is becoming more toned and I am looking better. I am attractive and feel sexy. I can eat better. I eat only when I'm hungry. I drink lots of fluids. When I eat, I choose healthy foods. etc . . . "

Notice how with this guideline, I chose words that felt comfortable to me. I didn't say "My waist is smaller now," because this statement wouldn't have been true. Write each suggestion as if it were true and present, but if it feels too unreal, then honor your feelings. Be aware though, that your beliefs may limit you. If you're not sure just how empowered to make your suggestions, then err on the side of too much. You can always cut it back if you don't like it. I can write, "My waist is becoming smaller." With all your suggestions, too much is better than too little. In the upcoming exercises, you will get a chance to feel the power of your suggestions in trance. Then you'll know what needs to be changed. You may be surprised how good these positive suggestions feel. After experiencing them, you may want to stretch yourself a little more!

Using guideline #3, affirm action not ability, I would change "I can.." to "I am." Then using guideline #4, Be detailed, I would put in the specifics about what kinds of food I would eat, how much I would exercise, and what kind of clothing I would wear.

As you continue working through each of the guidelines, your auto-suggestion will become clearer, stronger and more effective. Each guideline will help you think clearly about your goal. The more conscious focus you put into your intent, the more effective your self-hypnosis will become. Clearly, this takes some time and effort. It's worth it.

Here's my example following the guidelines (after multiple times and lots of re-writing):

Dancing in light.

I am dancing into a lighter place. I am becoming lighter in my heart and body and I feel great. I am eating a healthy diet and feeling more in control of my life. I am eating only natural foods, including lots of greens and grains. I enjoy the taste of these healthier foods and I feel better eating them. I know to stop when I'm not hungry any more. I enjoy knowing I am becoming healthier. I am losing weight as I'm dancing in my own inner lightness.

As I feel better, I am drinking four to six glasses of water, tea, and juice each day. Anytime I feel uncomfortable feelings, I drink some water, I breathe deeply and I relax. I take care of myself in a healthy way. I remind myself, "I'm okay. I can take care of myself." I allow myself to feel my emotions. It's okay for me to feel and to let go. I am strong and able to take care of myself emotionally and physically.

I go for short walks every day through the park and around my neighborhood. I enjoy how my body feels. I enjoy longer walks when I have extra time. I ride my bicycle three times each week. I feel energized and calmed every time I exercise. I am more in my body in a healthy way. I feel better about myself.

I am more confident about my looks. I feel attractive to myself and to others. I am a good person and I know it. I am more fit and full of light. As I'm more comfortable in my body, I feel more confident meeting people. I know I'm attractive as my inner light shows through my healthy, light body. I fit into my clothes easier and will easily fit into my old comfortable jeans by my birthday. On that day I will be 25 pounds lighter and I will feel truly comfortable in myself and in my body. I feel great. My body is more toned and vibrant. I am confident, excited to be me, excited to be alive! I am dancing in the light of my being.

All the healthy changes I'm experiencing make me excited to be alive. I am living my life filled with light, dancing with light, in light. I am eating at regular meal times and enjoying the healthy food I eat. Whenever I eat, I stop when I'm full. I am satisfied and in control of myself. As I become lighter, I am more in control of my life. My friends and family see me in control and feeling better. They see me as I am, filled with light and energy, dancing my life!

I am dancing in light.

Can you feel the energy and clarity of these words? Writing and refining your suggestion will do much toward making your goal real and tangible. As you get into the writing of it, you will feel the movement and energy of your intention. It's okay if you don't believe everything you are saying consciously, or if it feels a little too optimistic. Your words aren't for your conscious mind. Wait until you work with your auto-suggestion in hypnosis; then you'll experience how effective these words are. As you can see, it's okay to repeat important words or ideas. Also, be thorough with your suggestion. You might notice how I tend to use more feeling words in my suggestion. This is because I am strongly kinesthetic. So, when you write yours, be sure to emphasize your favorite senses. The more you engage with your goal and elaborate on the results you will experience, the more effective your self-hypnosis practice will be.

Rewrite your auto-suggestion.

Now spend some time rewriting your suggestions. On the next page is a summary of the guidelines. Take some time, look at each idea you put down, and refine it following the guidelines. Really work at it; you're worth it! With each sentence you have, explore ways to make it clearer and more concrete. Make sure to add feelings. With each statement you make, ask yourself, "How does this make me feel?" Then add those feelings. They are important.

Also, be sure to add details on how the changes you envision will actually affect your life. Ask yourself how you will experience changes. "How do I see myself being this way?" "How do I hear myself talking?" "How does my behavior change?" Add the details. Keep rewriting it as you go through each guideline. Emphasize your key words. Remember, even your best working draft doesn't have to be perfect. You can always revise as needed. When you have your auto-suggestion fine-tuned, write or type it clearly on a clean sheet of paper. You will use this working draft to do the next exercises in this workbook.

Appendix C has many more examples of finished auto-suggestions written by people who've taken my classes. Feel free to use ideas, words, and phrases from any of these suggestions as you refine your own, but put them in your own words. Make sure you include how achieving your goal will affect your life, your relationships, your work, your body, your health, your spirit, and even how you talk, walk, think and behave.

Once you've finished refining your auto-suggestion, you will have an opportunity to begin using it with the next self-practice in the next chapter.

Auto-suggestion Guidelines

1- Be positive.

2- Use present tense-present progressive - "I am . . ." or "You are . . ." or "I am becoming . . ."

3- Affirm action, not ability - not "I can . . ." but "I walk each day."

4- Be detailed. Think it through and be specific.

5- Use your own words and language.

6- Be realistic with numbers, amounts and actual activity.

7- Exaggerate and emotionalize feelings, senses, and the results of actions.

8- Time limit for suggestion: When will it be?

9- Repetition can be good: Reemphasize key concepts.

10 - Establish key words, a key phrase or a symbol that captures the essence of your intentions.

11 - Include details on how achieving your goal will actually affect your life.

Chapter 8
Self-Talk, Self-Control

Our intention creates our reality.
Wayne Dyer

Exercise five - deepening with key words

Did you make it through the entire refinement process? If so, congratulate yourself. Writing an effective auto-suggestion is an important step in your personal transformation. Taking the time and energy to clearly and concisely visualize your goal propels you toward your goal. You sent an important message to your subconscious about your seriousness. Your subconscious is already working on your goal.

Now that you have a working auto-suggestion tailored to your own specific goals, and you've had an introduction to the experience of hypnosis, you're ready to start combining your conscious and subconscious intentions into one practice. You will use your complete auto-suggestion before beginning this exercise and you will use the key words you selected in the middle of your induction.

You will use a variation of the deepening technique from the last guided exercise. This exercise uses, "You are . . . ", but feel free to change it to "I am . . . " if you prefer working with first person. Like the arm drop exercise earlier, speak the words aloud to yourself. Let your voice soften as you follow the feeling inwards. You can speak on the in-breath. Let the flow of your breath guide the flow of the words you speak. Make sure to give yourself time with the words. Let . . . your . . . mind . . . slow down . . . as you . . . read.

You will begin by reading your auto-suggestion. You may feel that your auto-suggestion still needs refinement, but as you read it this time enjoy the sound of the words and how they feel. Emphasize your key words at the beginning and end. Read the completed auto-suggestion aloud.

Deepening with key words - self direction.
Materials needed - journal, key words and auto-suggestion
Time - 20 minutes.

Read your auto-suggestions.
Then, read the following aloud to yourself, slowly, with attention:

> Now, (your name), sit comfortably so you can breathe easily and read these words softly to yourself without straining.
>
> In a few moments, I'm going to begin counting slowly from ten down to one.
>
> As I count, you will feel your body relax again, and you will return to a comfortable, light trance state.
>
> As each number drifts by, you can hear another part of your mind repeating the number, like an echo . . . relaxing you.
>
> You may also see the number drift through your inner vision, taking you into a more comfortable place.
>
> The deeper you go, the more comfortable and safe you become.
>
> At the count of one you will settle into a light trance state.
>
> As I count you down, allow each number to coincide with your exhaling breath, taking you deeper. Every time you see and hear a number, you can allow whatever breath you have in your body to flow easily out of you, relaxing you . . . and you can say the number with the end of your breath.
>
> So, beginning now with . . . .
>
> Ten . . . exhaling.
>
> Letting go . . . hearing the number echo inside inside your mind, allowing all muscles of your face to loosen up and relax . . . and spreading through your eyes, your nose and mouth . . . your jaw.
>
> Nine . . . a relaxing calmness easing down through all the muscles in your neck.
>
> Eight . . . and down into all the muscles and nerves in your shoulders . . . more and more relaxed, deeper and deeper.
>
> Seven . . . down . . . drifting through your chest and upper back, deeply and comfortably.

Six . . . echoing softly inside and spreading into your upper arms.

Five . . . flowing down with each sinking breath into your forearms, into your hands and all the way out the tips of your fingers.

Four . . . continuing . . . flowing down through the center of your body, into your abdomen and lower back, deeper and calmer.

Three . . . letting the relaxation spread down through your pelvis and your groin, front and back, flowing down into your legs, and your knees.

Two . . . flowing down through your lower legs, all the way down to your feet and the tips of your toes.

One . . . all the way down, much deeper, letting your whole body relax deeply, melting away any remaining tension and smoothing out, deeper and completely relaxed.

That's good Even with your eyes open . . . feeling just right inside, more and more comfortable, safe and relaxed.

Now, (your name) say your keywords to yourself softly . . . (keywords).

Enjoy the feeling of these key words without needing to do anything . . . and let your mind drift.

Say your keywords again, softly . . . (keywords).

Your subconscious is remembering all the other thoughts and feelings connected with your key words.

You can drift for a few moments more . . . remembering other positive feelings . . . not needing to do anything more.

(Pause as long as feels comfortable. You can repeat your keywords if you like.)

In a moment I'm going to count up from One to Five. When I reach Five, you will return to your normal consciousness. You will remember what you've learned and experienced in this pleasant trance state.

Beginning, counting up to . . .

One. Starting to come out of trance.

Two. More aware and alert . . . coming into your breathing.

Three. More aware and awake now, returning to normal, beginning to move your fingers and toes.

Four. Almost there, sensing the room around you.

Five. All the way back to normal consciousness.

End reading aloud.

Personal responses

While this experience is still fresh in your mind, answer the following questions:

1 - What are you feeling or experiencing now?

2 - Think how you felt prior to beginning this exercise. Do you feel any change now that you've completed it?

3 - Did you enjoy using counting and breathing as the deepening? Did you find it interesting in some way, or was it difficult? Was it helpful for you?

4 - What was your experience when you brought your keywords to mind in the middle of your trance process?

Discussion

Reading through your auto-suggestion before doing your trance practice will set your intention for the exercise. Your subconscious will pick up on all of your conscious thoughts and respond to them. The same is true for your key words. You may bring your key words to mind at any time during your trance process. Each time you say them to yourself, your subconscious will respond; there's nothing else you need to do consciously. You don't need to figure out how things will work themselves out or how the changes you're focusing on will occur. "Figuring" is a conscious process and only interferes with the intelligence of the subconscious. Bringing your key words to mind, you are releasing your intentions to your subconscious mind.

While you are in trance, images, feelings or even insights may arise in response to your intention and your key words. These are subconscious responses. Allow these spontaneous movements to happen, even if you feel they alert you a little. Your subconscious will respond energetically to your key words and intentions. With experience, you will learn to differentiate between these subconscious movements and your analytical thought processes. Allow your subconscious guidance to move you toward transformation. You may see yourself doing a helpful, positive activity, vividly in your inner vision, or you may clearly feel a different sensation in your body. Sensing your subconscious guidance and allowing it, can be very exciting.

Every time you do any self-hypnosis practice, check in with your feelings and thoughts afterwards. When you consciously recognize changes you've experienced, you validate your self-hypnosis process. Also, each time you do an exercise, you will better understand which parts worked well, which didn't and even which parts surprised you. Then, when you practice again, you can change your process to better suit you.

Notes on the awakening

Regardless how deep or profound your trance experience, it's important to finish with a bit of formal structure. The awakening is the closing structure of self-hypnosis. With the induction, deepenings and suggestions, you are choosing when you want to experience trance, what you want it to be like, and how long you want it to last. The awakening teaches you how to exit trance and return to a normal awakened state. As with the inductions, you can direct your consciousness to the specific state you want.

If you're practicing at night and you want to go to sleep afterwards, you can bring yourself to enough consciousness to finish your preparation for sleep. You could say, "When I reach five, I'll be in my normal consciousness again, but very comfortable and sleepy. I'll drift easily to sleep after I've brushed my teeth." If you're practicing in the middle of the day and you want to awaken energized, you could say, "I'll be filled with energy and be wide awake and alert when I reach the number five." You can also give yourself very specific suggestions to let positive feelings or insights you've gained in trance stay with you as you return to your normal state of consciousness, "When I reach five, I'll remember all these positive feelings. I'll remember who I really am." You don't ever have to leave behind the positive gains you've made in trance. You can carry them with you.

The awakening is a powerful component of the self-hypnosis process for shifting your consciousness. You can use a simple awakening to reenergize yourself any time you feel tired, a little sluggish, or out-of-focus. There's a fairly simple way to do this. Start by recognizing that you are tired. Take a deep breath and close your eyes for a moment. Acknowledge what you are experiencing. "I am feeling sluggish . . ." Then, when you feel present and inwardly connected, tell yourself you are going to count up to five and when you reach five you'll be awake and alert. Then count yourself up. As you count up, consciously activate your energy. Make a point of breathing deeply, stretching, moving, and thinking exciting thoughts. Come back into your body, your senses, and your breath. Be aware that you can modify the awakening to better suit you. If you're not where you want to be at the number five, then give yourself more numbers to come back or repeat the process.

With practice, your awakening can become just as quick and effective as your induction to trance. Each aspect of the trance process, from induction to awakening, gives you more control over your life. When you need to relieve stress or tension, you can calm and relax your whole being. When you're feeling down and need energy, you can use self-hypnosis to become more alert and aware.

In the next chapter, when you do your own self-hypnosis practice, you will use your auto-suggestions as you did for this last exercise. You will read through them before trance, then use your key words while you're in trance. This allows you to stay in trance without engaging your conscious mind. Later, as you become more familiar with trance, you will bring more and more of your intention to mind while you're experiencing hypnosis. Eventually you will be able to read through your complete auto-suggestion while you are in a deep trance. For now, just bringing your key words to mind allows your subconscious to work with them.

Chapter 9
Daily Practice and Affirmation

Your prosperity consciousness is not dependent on money; your flow
of money is dependent on your prosperity consciousness. As you can
conceive of more, more will come into your life.
Louise Hay

Independent practice

Now you're ready to practice independently. With a completely self-guided process you get to experience self-hypnosis in its most enjoyable form. Until now, you've always had to follow a script. Without a script, you can respond directly to what's happening in your mind and body and use those changes as part of your process. For example, during the eye fixation, when your eyes close, you can move right on to the next step. Whatever you experience, becomes the next step in your self-hypnosis process. Only when you are guiding yourself are you truly doing "self" hypnosis. While you may not feel ready to proceed without a script, remember you already have all the tools you need to practice on your own. Anytime you feel you need backup, the scripts are always available.

The first few times you practice self-hypnosis, you will use the process outlined on page 87. This starts with a basic check-in to get in touch with what you are presently experiencing. Then you describe what your goals are for the session. You will always have your primary focus and auto-suggestion with each exercise you do, but you can also address a specific intent. You may want to reenergize, calm down, or just get centered again.

Then you can decide which induction and deepenings you are going to use. The basic inductions and deepenings are briefly summarized beginning on page 88. Feel free to review your choices before you do your practice. (Examples of inductions and deepenings are written in full in Appendix D.) Be sure to use techniques you enjoy and use senses that come easily to you. There are some inductions and deepenings on the list you haven't experienced yet. Feel free to try them on your own, although you will get to experience them as you progress through the book. Write your key words on the form.

Once you've filled out the top part of the form, you are to do the exercise the way you've laid it out for yourself. As you do your practice, talk to yourself the way that works best for you, using either, "I am . . . " or "You are . . ."

Within the self-hypnosis structure, you have the option to use your key words more than once and to do more deepenings. After you have deepened enough to know you are in trance, bring your key words to mind and let your subconscious respond. Enjoy whatever happens and allow yourself to let go. Then, when you feel like being active again, do another deepening with more key words. If you have time, you can repeat this process several times. Each time you go deeper, your keywords and auto-suggestions go deeper into your subconscious.

You also have the option of reading your auto-suggestion while you're in trance. With practice, you can open your eyes and read while staying in trance. At the beginning, I recommend that you read your auto-suggestion before your trance; use just the key words in trance.

When you are finished with your practice, finish the form on the next page by answering the remaining questions. The follow-up questions will help you assess how it went. Make multiple copies of the practice form for your daily practice.

Exercise six - first self practice

Materials needed - practice form, key words and auto-suggestion.
Time needed - 30 to 40 minutes.

Make a copy of the form on the next page. Answer the questions and enjoy your first practice session. When you're finished with the form, take a break. Do something positive and fun for yourself.

Self-hypnosis Practice Form   Date:_____   Time:_____

Briefly describe the state of your mind, your body, and your emotions.

Are there any specific goals you would like to achieve now with this self-hypnosis session?

How long do you intend to practice this session of self-hypnosis?

Fill in the blanks below. Choose Inductions and deepenings from the list on the next page.

Preparation - Find a comfortable place where you can relax. Turn off the telephone and eliminate other distractions. Tell yourself how long you are going to practice self-hypnosis and what your intentions are.

Read your auto-suggestions. Read with a receptive frame of mind, not revising. Enjoy the sounds of the words and the feelings they create in your body.

Induction - _____

Deepenings - _____ and _____

Key words - _____

Awakening - Instruct yourself how in a few moments you will count yourself out from One to Five. Tell yourself what you will experience when you reach Five. Be specific. Then count up and bring yourself out.

Now do the whole process. If you forget what comes next, refer to this form for assistance. Remember to use pacing and leading. Also use, "I am feeling . . . and I'm okay" with any emotion. When finished, answer the remaining questions.

Briefly describe your current state of mind, body, and the emotions you feel.

How did the techniques you chose work for you?

How long did your self-hypnosis last?

Describe anything you enjoyed or learned from this practice session?

Describe any difficulties you had with this session?

Did your experience help you move towards your goal?

Inductions briefly summarized
Can also be used as deepenings.

Arm drop - Hold one arm out horizontally, close your eyes and relax. Imagine holding a bucket filling with water. Use all your senses. Encourage and allow the feelings that arise. Tell yourself what you will experience when the arm touches down. Pace and lead yourself, comment on what you are experiencing as you are moving towards your goal. Allow your breathing to work with you.

Eye-fixation - Focus your gaze on a spot. Choose a higher spot to create more eye fatigue. Enjoy the flow of your breath. Suggest that changes in your vision and body will start to occur naturally. Tell yourself what you will experience when the eyes close. Suggest heaviness in the eyelids. Pace and lead yourself, commenting on your experience as you lead toward your goal.

Counting down with breath - Instruct yourself that you will count from a number of your choosing down to one. Tell yourself what you will experience when you reach one. Synchronize your breathing with your counting; say one number at the end of every breath or every other breath. Using pacing and leading with any other feelings or sensations you experience. Enjoy the feeling and the sound of the numbers in your mind as you go deeper.

Stairway with counting - Instruct yourself to vividly imagine a stairway either going up or down. Tell yourself what will happen when you reach the end of the stairs. Then count yourself from twenty down to one as you go one step at a time to either the top or the bottom of the stairs. Use pacing and leading with any other feelings or sensations you experience. Use your full senses with the stairs and remember the feeling of traversing stairs.

Hand levitation - Choose your left or right hand and arm to levitate. Focus your awareness on your hand and arm and what you are sensing there. Begin to suggest a lightness, a tingling, a sense of expansion, and other sensations. Suggest lightness developing in the hand. Allow the hand and arm to become lighter and begin to lift up. As this happens, tell yourself what will happen as the arm levitates. Enjoy the experience and pace and lead towards your goal. As the arm is raising, tell yourself the hand will start moving towards the head with a magnetic force. Suggest the sensation of that force and attraction. Tell yourself what you will experience when the hand touches the head. Then allow the hand to drop back down and let go.

Progressive relaxation - Beginning with your feet, work your way up through your body, tightening muscle groups, holding tension, then releasing the tension. Repeat each muscle group two or three times. Instruct yourself how with each wave of tension and relaxation you will become more relaxed and comfortable. This induction is very helpful if you are tense to begin with or if you are experiencing stress in your body.

Deepenings briefly summarized

Counting down with relaxation - Instruct yourself that you will count from a number of your choosing down to one. Tell yourself what you will experience when you reach one. Synchronize your breathing with your counting - one number for every breath or one with every other breath each time you get to the end of an exhale. Relax your body with each number, going down through your body as you go down to one. You can imagine a relaxing color flowing down through your body as well.

Positive place and senses - Bring a positive place to mind, either real or imaginary. Engage all your senses in the positive feelings and memories of this place. Tell yourself as you do this, what end result you will experience. Bring to mind specific senses you enjoy - sounds, images, feelings, smells and emotions. Allow your imagination and creativity to work for you.

Quiet time - Instruct yourself that you will let yourself drift and your subconscious will guide you. Tell yourself what you will experience as this happens. Then, let go. No other structure is needed. You can allow your conscious mind to drift.

Discussion

Congratulations. You've successfully gone through your first independent self-hypnosis experience. Regardless how "deep" you went into hypnosis or how effective you feel you were, going through the process by yourself is an important step. Each time you practice, you will become more familiar with trance and the process of hypnosis. By now, after doing all the previous exercises, you have a sense of what the trance state feels like. It's important to validate your own experiences. Recognizing what is happening builds a much stronger connection to your subconscious.

On that note, also remember to use pacing and leading. If you are counting down and feel an emotion or a body sensation, welcome it into your awareness. Lead yourself into the next part of your induction. Pacing and leading are especially powerful with unexplained or irrational feelings and sensations. They come directly from the subconscious and, by validating them, your connection to the subconscious becomes stronger. Then, your leading and intention becomes more effective.

Here are some comments from students regarding their beginning practice sessions:

"I enjoyed the ease of the deepening (going to a positive place) and the simplicity of it. I'm pleased with the positive results. The joy I feel helps bring my true self, love. I'm reassured that I can feel okay. I feel stronger."

"I felt good about the eye-fixation and the counting down, but didn't stay there. I experienced a lot of bouncing in and out. I think next time I will try more structure and not use 'quiet time.' I need more guidance."

"I did feel and see better than I did being guided which surprised me, as I thought I would have done much better being led."

"I do feel rested, calm and, at the moment, more centered. Even if I did drift off, I feel good that I got there and especially since my mind was quite active when I sat down."

As you read your auto-suggestion through before this session, how did it feel? How did the key words make you feel in trance? Here's how some students experienced their auto-suggestion:

"It is easier to own my suggestions in trance. They feel more comfortable."

"Everytime I hear my auto-suggestion I feel it's more true. When I wrote it, it felt like wishful thinking, but now it's becoming more real. I can see why it's good to repeat it many times. It's easy to lose it during the day."

Each time you read your auto-suggestion now, your words will resonate deep inside you. If you feel a need to change or alter your auto-suggestion, take more time to revise it before you do your next practice session. Feel free to add more detail and feeling. You can also change your key words if you need to. You want these words to capture the essence of the intent you are focusing on. Be sure to keep your most current version of your auto-suggestion on hand when you practice.

When you feel comfortable with your auto-suggestion, stop working on it. Let it be as it is. Your subconscious will work with all the intention you've put into it. Then, when you read it, enjoy the sound and feelings of the words, more like a poem. Your "feeling" body will enjoy the words and respond.

Affirmations

So far you've learned three simple ways to work with suggestions and affirmations. First, you can pace and lead with a feeling, "I am feeling (your feeling) and I'm okay." This can be done in trance or throughout the day. Second, you can use your auto-suggestion before your self-hypnosis practice. Third, you can also use your key words during trance. Each of these techniques help you consciously keep your intention focused on your goals.

Now, I'll show you a way you can use your keywords and suggestions throughout the day as affirmations. You can pause wherever you are and hear and see your key words inside your mind. Let yourself breathe, and pause a moment longer to enjoy the feeling of your words. Then resume whatever you were doing, and enjoy feeling a little better. You already have lots of intention put into your key words. They will have more and more affect as you use them more frequently.

You can also use individual sentences from your auto-suggestion as daily affirmations. Here's the first part of the auto-suggestion I used earlier as an example:

I am dancing into a lighter place. I am becoming lighter in my heart and body and I feel great. I am eating a healthy diet and feeling more in control of my life. I am eating only natural foods, including lots of greens and grains. I enjoy the taste of these healthier foods and I feel better eating them. I know to stop when I'm not hungry any more. I enjoy knowing I am becoming healthier. I am losing weight as I'm dancing in my own inner lightness. As I feel better, I am drinking lots of water, teas, and juices. Anytime I feel uncomfortable feelings, I drink some water. I breathe deeply and relax. I take care of myself in a healthy way. I remind myself, "I'm okay, I can take care of myself." I allow myself to feel my emotions. It's okay for me to feel and to let go. I am strong and able to take care of myself emotionally and physically.

I would pick several lines I felt strongly about and use one of them as an affirmation for each day of the week. Here's what I would use from my example:

Sunday - I am dancing into a lighter place.

Monday - I am strong and able to take care of myself emotionally and physically.

Tuesday - I enjoy knowing I am becoming healthier.

Wednesday - It's okay for me to feel and let go.

Thursday - I am taking care of myself in a healthy way.

Friday - I am becoming lighter in my heart and body.

Saturday - I am losing weight as I'm dancing in my own inner lightness.

Pick seven phrases from your auto-suggestion you would like to instill deeper in your subconscious. Then, each morning when you get up, write your phrase for the day down on a piece of paper in your date book, or even on your hand. Put it somewhere you'll see it. Every time you see the phrase, pause a moment, and say it to yourself. Feel the energy behind your words. Your positive words become affirmations, keeping you in touch with your intentions throughout the day. Your affirmations add power to your self-hypnosis practice. You will find, with practice, how each phrase comes automatically and becomes part of you. Your own words are much more effective than affirmations from a book. They feed your soul and energize you. With your personal suggestions in your mind, you will begin acting in a positive way.

Write your list of affirmations. Post them somewhere you'll see them in the morning. Use them.

Night time reminder

Once you have your phrases for each day, choose the most exciting and empowering one from your list. Write that sentence on an index card. Place the card next to your bed. When you go to bed each night, read the affirmation to yourself as you drift toward sleep. Repeat it several times. Ideally you want this phrase to be the last thing in your mind as you are going to sleep. The content of your mind, as you enter into sleep, becomes an extremely strong suggestion to your subconscious. Your phrase will carry with you through the whole night, working for you as you sleep.

Read this suggestion each night before bed for three or four weeks. Make a practice of it and your subconscious will get the message loud and clear. For more effect, you can write your affirmation on larger papers, large enough to read from a distance, and pin the sentence on the ceiling above your bed. Gaze at your words as you drift into the sleep state.

Fill your mind with your positive intentions. Your affirmation will be the last thing you see each time you turn out the lights.

Daily practice

Now you are ready for more self-hypnosis practice. Continue using the practice form to guide your sessions. Vary the inductions and the deepenings until you get a sense which ones work best for you. Some may work better in the morning or evening. Other combinations may work better if you are feeling a little stressed. Remember, the physical inductions, like the arm drop and eye-fixation, work well if you are feeling stressed. They give you something tangible to start with. Feel free to improvise your own deepenings and inductions. Like the stairway induction, you might imagine being in another place, moving, walking, or even drifting in a boat or on a cloud. Any sensation of movement you've experienced can become an induction or a deepening.

Do one or two practice sessions each day for one week. Be sure to practice at different times of the day. You may find it easier to relax and enter hypnosis at one time of day, but you may need it more at another time. Also, if you fall asleep when practicing, then pick a time when you are rested. If you're too energized, pick a calmer time. Be sensitive to your needs. If you have some extra time in the middle of the day, use it. Keep your auto-suggestion with you and read it before a short rest in the middle of the day.

Be aware of self-imposed limitations. You may think it takes twenty minutes, a comfortable chair and a quiet environment to practice, but you can break all those rules. If you only have 10 minutes in the middle of a busy day, then do one simple induction or deepening, bring your keywords to mind, then let yourself go right back to your normal routine. You can even do a brief, eyes open induction in the middle of a crowded cafeteria. The shortest induction would involve bringing your key words to mind as you are moving about through the day.

Fill out a copy of the practice form for each of your practice sessions. The form will help you discover more about yourself as you practice in different settings and situations. When you do a spontaneous session in a busy environment, you'll understand how effective it can be.

As you do this week's practice, feel free to review the earlier parts of the manual. As your experience deepens, parts of the text will resonate differently with you. The next chapters will go deeper into trance, exploring other forms of induction and deepening, and specific ways you can apply it to your life. As you continue reading, be sure to continue your self-hypnosis practice.

I'm okay

Chapter 10
Deeper Into Relaxation

When I'm trusting and being myself . . . everything in my life reflects this by
falling into place easily, often miraculously.
Shakti Gawain

Becoming more comfortable with trance

Effective self-hypnosis works through a balance of conscious and unconscious intentions. Ideally, both these aspects of your psyche are working together, each doing what it does best and not interfering with the other. The conscious, critical mind is ideally suited for handling new stimulus and situations. With conscious thought, you make decisions, reach logical conclusions, and respond to needs that arise. In the practice of self-hypnosis, you consciously envision the changes you want to manifest. The subconscious is much better suited to managing all the other elements not needing your conscious focus. Creative and intuitive modes of thinking come through the subconscious as does functioning of the body, healing, sleep processes, and regular routine actions. A healthy marriage between the conscious and subconscious mind generates a greater sense of well-being.

Learning to trust the feeling of a movement from the subconscious can be very valuable. As you gain familiarity with yourself, you can allow some illogical feelings, knowing they are congruent with your deeper intentions. Sometimes these illogical actions are more effective than any actions you could take with conscious direction. A feeling of heaviness behind your eyes and a wandering mind are not logical. But, with familiarity, you recognize them as signals of tiredness. If you allow them to lead you to a brief nap you can return to a more energized state afterwards.

Have you felt any changes since you've been practicing? Since trance is inherently relaxing, the self-hypnosis process teaches you how to release stress quickly and to avoid creating more tension in your life. Moving in and out of trance also creates a healthier flexibility in your body and mind. You have more energy available when you need it. You can be more alert when you need to be. Instead of fighting against yourself, you start to flow with your inner intuitive knowing.

At some point, most likely after a week's practice and refining, your auto-suggestion won't need further refining. Then, each time you read it, you can allow the words to flow through your mind and your body with a rhythm of their own, like a familiar song. The intention in your words will spark a deeper, creative process. You will find yourself creatively embodying your intentions in your daily life. The behavior you envision in your suggestion will start showing up in small effortless ways. Your intentions will even start flowing into other aspects of your life. Your dreams will start changing as your subconscious responds. Your daydreams will lead you to more spontaneous insights into your process. You may feel a subtle message-- a feeling, a knowing or an image -- guiding you in the middle of the day. You'll find yourself actually living the images you've created.

Here are more comments from students regarding changes they've experienced after a week of practice.

"Well, I didn't really do my practice the last few days. At one point I had to stand up and speak in front of 200 people, and I just got up there, no problem. My body wasn't nervous. I felt confident. I didn't speak for long, but my family and friends told me what I said was just perfect. So, I feel like I did do my homework, but it was in a different way than I expected."

"I feel the most successful with the critical voice in my head. I am allowing things to come. There isn't anything wrong. In the past, when I tried to meditate, I'd hear the dog barking two blocks away and I'd be distracted. Turning these distractions into a positive thing, allowing them, has really helped me."

"I have become more aware of my body, when it's relaxed and when it's not relaxed. Being at the dentist's office this morning, I was more aware of my body. I felt less stress."

"When things happen to me at work, which is very stressful, I am more able to handle it. I deal with it better without panic or anxiety. I feel like work is a lot easier."

"I like going inside and letting everything else go. Voices and things from the day go away and it feels like I'm transported to another place. I feel like I'm a different person. I think it's the relaxation that comes and goes through my whole body. I don't even have to think about each place to relax. The feeling just comes by itself. It happens."

You will experience your own changes as the people in the above examples did. You may have difficulties some days. Other days your practice may flow easily and your day may go smoothly. The inductions you use may shift as you learn other, more appropriate techniques. In the end, it isn't the specific techniques that matter, it's your capacity to look within and move into a deeper connection with yourself. What you access with trance is a completely natural part of who you are. You can continue to expand your own consciousness within the daily living of your life.

As you practice self-hypnosis more, you will start to sense some times when it's easier to go into trance and some times when it's more difficult. This difference may be due to the way your energy cycles through the day or to general levels of stress or tension you're feeling. If you are feeling a little tense, it might take more intent to shift and enter into trance. If you are relaxed to begin with, shifting is easier. Practicing during your tense times will teach you more self-control and confidence. You can intentionally shift to a more relaxed place in the middle of a highly stressful experience. You can be in control wherever you are and whatever you're experiencing. You can take care of yourself.

This next exercise will be directed entirely at your body. It is very useful when you are experiencing physical stress or tension.

Exercise seven - progressive relaxation

First, find a relaxed position, preferably lying down or sitting comfortably. Then read through the script to get a sense of how progressive relaxation works. You will see it is a fairly simple technique. Then set the book down and go through the whole body tightening and relaxing technique. Feel free to isolate the muscle groups in different ways to suit your body.

Materials needed - journal and key words.
Time needed - 30 minutes.

As you relax and settle down, allow your breathing to fall into a comfortable rhythm, not too fast, not too slow.

In a few moments, you will tighten and hold tension in different muscle groups in your body. You will hold the tension in your muscles firmly without straining yourself. Then, when you let go of the muscles, you can let go and relax completely.

To begin, tighten all the muscles in your feet. Let your feet curl up as the muscles tighten. Feel the pressure and tension . . . hold it . . . then let go.
Relax completely. Let all the muscles in the feet relax.
Breathe easily and naturally.
One more time now, tighten all the muscles in your feet.
Tense every muscle you can . . . hold that tension.
Let it go. Let all the muscles relax. Enjoy the release of letting go.
Breathe easily and comfortably.

Next, tighten all the muscles in your lower legs and ankles. Parts of the feet may tighten again too. That's okay. Hold the tension.
Now let go, let all the muscles relax and smooth out.
Breathe easily.
Again, tighten all the muscles in your lower legs and ankles. Hold that tension . . . . then let go.
Let all those muscles smooth out and relax.
Breathe easily and naturally.

Now tighten the muscles in your upper legs, knees and buttocks. Let your body move if it needs to. Tighten all those large muscles. Hold the tension . . . then let go.
Let all those muscles relax and smooth out. Let all the tension drain away.
Breathe easily and peacefully.
Again, tighten all the muscles in the upper legs, knees, and buttocks. Front and back, inside and out. Hold that tension . . . then let them go.
Let all the tension drain away. Relax completely.
Breathe easily and comfortably.
Be aware of the sensations in your legs now. You can remember the feeling of deep relaxation.
Notice how the muscles feel.
Breathe comfortably.

Now we'll continue, moving up the body.
Tighten all the muscles in your lower torso, lower abdomen, back, and buttocks. Tighten

them all. Inside and out. Let your body move if it needs to. Hold them tight . . . then let them go.

All the muscles are relaxing and letting go. Allow all the tension to drain away. This feels so good.

Breathe easily and comfortably.

Again, tighten the lower part of your body again, all the muscles, inside and out, back and front, everything. Holding . . . then let them all go and relax.

Let all the tension drain away now.

Breathe easily and smoothly.

Moving up to the chest and the upper back, tighten all the muscles you can in your chest and shoulders, front and back, even into the neck. Tense your upper body. Hold that tension . . . then relax.

Let all the tension drain away. Relax all those muscles.

Breathe easier and easier.

Again, tighten all the muscles in your upper chest, shoulders, front and back, sides, and up into the neck. Holding . . . feeling the tension . . . then let go.

Let them all go. Relax completely. Let all the tension drain away.

And breathe easily and naturally.

Now move to your hands. Tense and tighten all the muscles in your hands. Make a fist, tense your wrists and forearms. Tense the end of your arm and hands. Holding tight, clenching . . . then let go.

Let all the muscles relax, and allow the tension to drain away.

Breathe easily and comfortably.

Again, make a fist with your hand, wrist and forearm. Allow all the muscles to tighten, building the tension.

You may even get some vibration in the arm from the tension.

Then let go. Let all the tension drain away.

Breathe easily and smoothly.

Next, moving to the upper arms. Tighten all the muscles, in your elbow, upper arm and shoulders. Your elbow may even bend. Hold all those muscles tight.

Then let go. Let them all relax and release . . . let all the tension flow out of your body.

Breathing easily and more relaxed.

Again, tighten the muscles of the upper arm, shoulders and elbow. Allow all those muscles to tense and tighten . . . hold that tension . . . then let it go.

Let all the muscles relax. They can smooth out and relax now.
Breathe easily in and out.

Now, moving up to the head, neck and face. Tighten all the muscles in your face,
    tightening the neck and jaw. The shoulders may move; that's okay. All holding,
    scrunching . . . then let go and relax.
Release all the tension.
Breathe easily and comfortably, letting go.
One more time, tighten all the muscles in your face, jaw and neck, holding all those
    muscles, scrunching. Feeling all the tension . . . holding it . . . then let go.
Let all the muscles relax now, and breathe easily and comfortably.

As you breathe now, easily, you feel so good, relaxed all over.
Be aware what you are feeling in your body.
This is the feeling of your relaxation.
Breathe in and out comfortably.
Enjoy your felt sense of relaxation.
Enjoy the deep peace in you.
Your body is relaxed now.
Bring your key words to mind and enjoy yourself.
Any time you want, you can repeat this process, going through your whole body.
You can repeat any areas still feeling tense or tight.
You can take care of yourself.
And now, you can energize yourself enough to bring yourself up to a normal state of
    consciousness.
End script.

Now repeat the whole process of progressive relaxation by yourself. Find a comfortable position where you can relax. Take as much time as you need to go through your whole body.

Personal responses

Take a few moments while this experience is fresh in your mind and answer these questions:

1 - What are you feeling now?

2 - What changes have you experienced in your body, mind or emotions as a result of this exercise?

3 - Was there anything interesting, surprising, or unusual occurring to you during this exercise?

Discussion

Progressive relaxation can be a very effective beginning to trance. As with other physical inductions, focus on your body will calm and release tension and stress in your mind. Having a calm, relaxed body will help you with other inductions or deepenings.

In self-hypnosis, you will become more aware of the guidance of the subconscious. Have you found yourself coming spontaneously out of trance in the middle of a session? There is a body intelligence guiding the flow of your conscious awareness. In hypnosis, this is called the ideomotor connection. "Ideo" refers to mind and "motor" refers to body or the physical part of us. The ideomotor is the mind/body connection as you experience it. Through the ideomotor connection, your subconscious can communicate what its intentions are. Have you found yourself feeling suddenly tired, say in the middle of the afternoon? Your subconscious is saying, "It's time to rest now," "Pay attention to your feelings," or something specific to you. Any body sensation arising by itself is an ideomotor signal coming directly from your subconscious.

> "It is helpful to have an induction into ourselves, to find the space that is trying to articulate. This reminds us that we have a communication line to ourselves and no one else can go there - unless we invite them there. This space inside is also the self. The ideomotor comes out of this space, my own space, and knowing that only I know."
> - Marlene Mulder, Hypnotherapy Training Institute

As you continue with your self-hypnosis practice, pay attention to the times your subconscious is leading you. The ideal time to go into trance is when your attention is already drifting. The ideal time to focus on an outward activity is when your body is energizing itself. As you learn to listen to the wisdom within you will gain a strong sense of self-confidence and trust. Next, with the second guided induction, you'll have an opportunity to build on the relaxation of your body and go deeper into trance.

key words

Chapter 11
A More Profound Connection

The physical world, including our bodies, is a response of the observer.
We create our bodies as we create the experience of our world.
Deepak Chopra

Exercise eight - second guided induction

Next, you will experience a deeper, more internal process of trance. For this exercise you will be guided again from a track on the CD. Being guided into hypnosis is much like getting a body massage. You receive something you know you want. With familiarity, you let yourself go and trust the process. When you're guided, you receive a meaningful gift.

Before you begin, bring to mind something specific you would like to experience. Here are some examples from students prior to this exercise:

"I want to feel self-acceptance."

"I want to feel well-being."

"I would like my throat to relax. It's been tight all week."

"I want to experience a new focus in my life."

"I want to feel a sense of accomplishment."

Notice how these statements don't say what they don't want. They address what each person is moving towards. Positive intention is important.

What do you want to experience? Write it down.

Each time you practice, you can directly address a feeling or a knowing you want to experience. When you have an intent, proceed with the next exercise. This induction will again go through all four stages of trance and will include your auto-suggestion and your key words.

Exercise Eight - second longer induction - CD exercise #3.
Materials - CD and player, auto-suggestion, key words.
Time needed - 45 minutes.

Find a comfortable place where you won't be disturbed for 45 minutes. Loosen any restrictive clothing you may be wearing and have your CD player on hand. Give yourself permission to enjoy this experience. Before turning on the CD, read through your auto-suggestion with an open and receptive mind. Then set your words aside and allow your subconscious to work with them. Take off your glasses. Remember what you wrote above to remind yourself what you want to experience. Answer the questions on page 110 and 111 after finishing the induction.

Begin CD.

Exercise eight - script.
    Now you can settle down and relax.
    As you listen to the sound of my voice you might wonder how you will experience
        another interesting and profound trance experience.
    As you relax, your subconscious is already rising up to meet you.
    At any time during this exercise you may go deeper, ahead of me, and that's fine.
    Remember what you wrote regarding what you want to achieve or experience.
    Then relax. You can attend to what's important to you.

Self-reporting scale introduction

A large part of learning to enter trance is just learning to trust your own experience.

One way of deepening self-awareness, is to imagine your awareness resides on a continuum, a scale that goes from 1 to 100.

The number 100 represents a state of being completely alert and aware, as in an extreme fight or flight situation.

Naturally this would be a place where you would only stay for a short time.

This is a state we very rarely experience, if ever.

At the other end of the scale, the number 1 might indicate being as deeply into your own subconscious as you can imagine, deeper even than in a deep sleep.

Imagining that kind of depth now, you may not even sense the possibility of it.

So now, ask yourself, "What number represents where I am on the scale?"

Notice the first number that pops into your mind.

Whatever number you perceive, just allow it, notice it, then let it go.

You can remember the number you perceived later.

The more you use the self-reporting scale, the easier and more spontaneous it becomes.

You can bring it to mind during the day while working, or while resting, and learn more about your consciousness.

With practice, your subconscious will instantly provide the relevant number when you ask.

Induction - stairs and counting

Now, as you relax, I want you to imagine you are surrounded by a mist and suspended with a very comfortable feeling.

In front of you are two staircases side by side, one extending upward into the mist, and one extending downward.

As you observe these staircases, you will feel a gentle pull toward one of them.

Your subconscious already knows which direction it would like to go.

Let it lead you.

Know you can always change directions if your subconscious desires a change.

Then, standing in front of the staircase you've chosen, notice how these stairs are carpeted in a thick plush carpet of your favorite color.

Imagine the carpet extending out from the stair under your feet.

If you're wearing any shoes, you can remove them and feel the soft, thick carpet squishing around your toes.

Also, on one side of you is a hardwood banister extending the length of the stairway.

You can easily place your hand on the banister and feel its strong, smooth texture.

In a few moments, I'm going to start counting from Ten down to One.

With each number I say, I'd like you to move forward one step at a time, letting the stairway lead you.

With each step you take, you can drift into a more comfortable feeling.

With each number, you can go deeper into trance, regardless if you are rising on your stairs or descending, until you reach the number one, all the way down . . . into a comfortable state of trance.

When I say deeper, you go into a more profound sense of trance, although you may even be feeling lighter as you go.

Enjoy your experience of trance.

Beginning now with . . .

Ten, letting go so easily.

As you take each step, feel the change in elevation.

Your body knows this feeling and remembers the feeling of the shift as you go deeper into trance.

Nine.

Enjoying the space in between each number . . . drifting.

Eight.

Feel free to add thoughts to yourself as you go deeper.

Seven.

Pacing and leading to yourself with what you are experiencing now.

Six.

Feeling so safe, so secure and comfortable.

Five.

Four.

Three.

Deeper relaxed with each step.

Two.

The deeper you go the better you feel.

One, all the way down into a comfortable sense of trance.

Deepening - sound of voice

You may even notice, as you continue drifting deeper, how my voice has become calmer and quieter and has developed the familiar rhythmic quality.

This rhythm will begin to accompany the sensations within your body allowing you to go deeper.

The rhythmic quality in my voice is actually connected to a pleasant rhythm that is inside of you, coming from deep within you.

In the same way, any time you add a thought to yourself, your own rhythm takes you deeper.

As all this occurs so easily, you may wonder, with a detached sense of curiosity, what number you are at now on the scale from 1 to 100.

Ask and see what comes.

Then let it drift away.

You can remember your numbers later if you want.

Deepening - escalator

From within this felt sense of relaxation, I'd like you to imagine yourself floating along, as if you were on a special kind of conveyor allowing you to drift forward as you are now, comfortably.

As you drift closer you can see there is a softly illuminated sign with a soft glow, hanging in the air above you.

The sign is pulsing the words "Deeper Relaxed".

As you pass under the sign, its light washes over you and relaxes your body.

Up ahead of you is another fork in the path.

At the fork there are two escalators this time, one going up and one going down.

Now, as you move closer to the escalators, you may even wonder which one will take you deeper relaxed in just the right way.

You drift now, allowing your subconscious to choose for you.

You find yourself moving in this comfortable way onto the right one.

The feeling of going deeper happens all by itself.

Now, moving forward, you can drift so comfortably, just carried along, not needing to do anything or trying not to do anything.

The escalator is connected to your own felt sense inside, taking you deeper.

Regardless of which escalator you are on, notice as you move forward your sense of depth increases all on its own.

Enjoy the felt sense of going deeper, lighter, easier, more comfortable and relaxed.

You may even notice comfortable rhythmic sounds accompanying you, guiding you deeper.

A part of you can sense the end of this escalator . . . far ahead . . . sensing the deep, calm place.

Let your awareness move into that feeling.

There is a wisdom inside you guiding you.

Enjoy the inner connection, allow yourself to drift as deep as you wish.

All the way into trance . . . toward the feelings that you want to manifest.

You may even notice with a detached sense of curiosity what number you are at now on the scale from 1 to 100.

Ask yourself . . . see what comes . . . then let it go.

Deeper relaxed and keywords

Now from within this felt sense of drifting and feeling so comfortable, you can engage more consciously with a word and idea.

When I say the words, "deeper relaxed," allow them to echo inside your mind.

See them on the screen of your inner vision.

Feel them resonate in your body . . . deeper relaxed.

As you feel and hear these words, your subconscious responds.

Say them again to yourself . . . deeper relaxed.

Now bring your key words to mind.

Hear and enjoy the sound of your words in the same way.

Let them resonate deep down in your being.

You may even see another softly illuminated sign drift by, washing you with your keywords, washing all the intentions behind those words deep into your body, taking you deeper.

You can let go and enjoy the feelings and images that come with your key words.

Your subconscious will lead you exactly where you need to go.

Pacing and leading to what you want

Now, from within your experience, find a word that describes what you are feeling. Allow the right word to come to mind.

Say to yourself, "I am feeling . . ." and add your word. Validate yourself.

Now this time, say to yourself, "As I am feeling . . . " your word . . . then add "I am becoming . . . " and add what you want now, what's important to you.

"I am feeling . . . and I am becoming . . . ."

Say the whole sentence to yourself, either aloud or inside your mind.

Say it again, softly to yourself, and feel the words resonating down through your whole body.

With this phrase, you validate yourself. You are okay right now, just the way you are.

You can recognize what you are feeling at any time of your day, and lead into what you want, "and I am becoming . . . ."

You will empower yourself each time you do so.

Deepening - Hypnodream

And as you continue drifting now, you may notice how even your imagination begins to free up, your mind drifting, your imagery is drifting, becoming more dreamlike.

Images, sensations, even thoughts drifting through your mind are taking on a dreamlike quality . . . changing, transforming, taking you along with them.

Enjoy this now as your subconscious leads you.

Wherever you go into this dreamlike flow, your subconscious will form within you just the right experience.

Now you can drift a few minutes as this dreamlike state unfolds.

As this voice becomes quiet for a few moments, you can let go.

(Pause.)

Suggestions

And now from wherever you are, your memories and experiences will stay with you.

You will be able to remember all the important experiences, images, sensations you've had.

You can also notice again what number would represent where you just were on the depth scale; just notice what number appears and feels right.

Each time you experience hypnosis, it gets easier and easier.

Each time, you learn more about yourself.

As you find this practice becoming more natural, you enjoy yourself more.

Your practice becomes comfortable and rewarding.

You can easily find the time to practice at home, or at work, or anywhere that feels just right.

Allowing the right amount of time to learn and understand in a deeper way.

You may even enjoy just a few moments of learning relaxation, easy remembering of new thoughts and ideas.

You are now taking charge of your life.

Feeling calm and relaxed, but also clear and strong, healthy and alive.

You are learning from experiencing inside your own feeling, your own felt sense of well-being.

Awakening

From whereever you are, in a few moments I'm going to count up from One to Five.

When I reach five, you will be awake, alert, refreshed, feeling good all over, and remembering what you experienced.

You'll find you can sleep very deeply and profoundly tonight and awaken refreshed in the morning as a result of this experience.

You'll find you'll have very vivid, colorful, and pleasant dreams you will be able to remember in the morning.

All right. You're able to come up now, coming up a little way to One.

Feelings starting to come back in your body, coming up a little more to Two.

Starting to move a little . . . fingers, toes . . . taking a deep breath.

Coming up a little more to Three, building your sense of your body and the room around you again.

Coming up a little more to Four.

Getting ready to come all the way back, coming all the way up to Five.

That's good. Stretch. Take a deep breath, and open your eyes when you're ready.

Turn off the CD and answer the questions in the manual.

End script.

Personal responses

Now take a few moments while this experience is fresh in your mind and answer these questions.

1. What are you feeling now?

2. What numbers appeared to you when you asked about your depth?

3. How did these numbers relate to or affect your experience?

4. What number on the depth scale are you now?

5. Was there anything interesting, surprising, or unusual you experienced during this exercise?

Now I would like you to consider each of the following parts to this induction. If there are parts you don't remember, that's okay, you may have been drifting deeper. Remember, if you want to be more aware, you can always repeat this exercise after you are rested or while sitting more upright.

6. Depth scale - You set up a scale from 1 to 100 to represent trance depth. Then you asked the subconscious periodically to indicate a depth. Did you enjoy this part, find it interesting in some way, or find it difficult? Was it helpful for you?

7. Stairway and counting - You imagined two stairways - one up, one down. You allowed your subconscious to choose one. Then, while counting, you used the stairs to go into trance. Did you enjoy this part, find it interesting in some way, or find it difficult? Was it helpful for you?

8. Rhythm of the voice - You focused consciously on the rhythm of the voice and allowed this same rhythm into your own inner experience. Did you enjoy this part, find it interesting in some way, or find it difficult? Was it helpful for you?

9. Escalator - You imagined two escalators - one up, one down. You allowed one escalator to take you deeper into trance. Did you enjoy this part, find it interesting in some way, or find it difficult? Was it helpful for you?

10. Keywords - You brought your keywords to mind, then allowed your subconscious to respond. Did you enjoy this part, find it interesting in some way, or find it difficult? Was it helpful for you?

11. Leading to what you want - You allowed a word to come to mind, describing what you were feeling. Then you added the words, "and I'm becoming" and what you wanted. You spoke the phrase, "As I am feeling (your word), I am becoming (your words)." Did you enjoy this part, or find it difficult? Was it helpful for you?

12. Hypnodream - You received suggestions for imagery, thoughts and sensations to become more dreamlike. Then you allowed your subconscious to lead you into a dreamlike experience. Did you enjoy this part, find it interesting in some way, or find it difficult? Was it helpful for you?

Discussion

If there were any parts of this induction that truly resonated with you, then go back and reread the script for that part. The scripts are there for you so you can incorporate them in your own practice.

This induction offered you an opportunity to go deeper into hypnosis with some quiet time for your own personal, subconscious responses. You can allow similar quiet periods in your own self-practice. You can also allow your subconscious to guide you with dreamlike, creative imagery. This style of induction works mostly with inward awareness and imagery. Since you are now more familiar with trance, you may be able to enter into trance more easily. Not using a physical induction technique as part of the self-hypnosis process, you relax your body beforehand by finding a comfortable position or doing a progressive relaxation. Then you go into trance entirely with imagery and inner focus. If you have a hard time relaxing your body or calming your mind at the start, then use one of the physical inductions.

During the induction and the deepening, you had the option of going up or down. Did you find yourself spontaneously going one direction? Did this surprise you? For some people going up feels more comfortable than going down. For others it's reversed. Allow yourself to go the way that feels best to you, not what you think is right. Your subconscious may even surprise you by leading in a different way than you expect. I recommend trying both directions at some point, to see what, if any, differences you experience. Like all the other aspects of trance, you may find your preferences changing at different times. You can trust your subconscious to lead you each time. Whatever your subconscious needs or wants to have happen will occur naturally. Here's how one student experienced the choice at the stairs:

> "I felt at first that I wanted to go down. There was a real nice dark area below. Then it was like my subconscious said, 'No, you're going up.' It felt like a separate directive from me. It was a little odd though, because it felt like there were two things going on in my head at the same time. I went up and yet I was getting deeper. I went into it fine, though it was very strange."

As with the the stairs and the escalator, there are many other ways you can use your imagination to go into trance. You can use any experience where you've sensed some kind of movement or transition. Other examples might include: riding an elevator, driving in a car, rocking in a hammock, drifting in a boat, floating on clouds, floating down a stream, descending down a mine-shaft or a tunnel, gliding on skis, or being rocked to sleep. If any of these examples evoke a pleasant memory, use them. Like all inductions or deepenings, tell yourself what you are going to do and what will occur as that happens. Then imagine the activity in your mind, feel the movement in yoru body, and enjoy the experience. If you like using numbers, you can add counting.

The more familiar you become with trance, you will start to notice times when you simply drift deeper into trance without any conscious leading. For instance, this may have happened during the last induction while I was counting down. There was a point when a few numbers came by with no other suggestions. There was also a point later with the dream suggestions when you were allowed to drift without leading. These were opportunities to let your subconscious lead. Periods of drifting, especially when they occur spontaneously, are times when your subconscious is directing you. When you experience yourself drifting, allow it. Suppose you are counting down and you forget all about the numbers for a few moments. Then at some point you remember where you are and realize you've been somewhere else. Say to yourself, "Thank you . . . Drifting deeper," and continue counting from where you left off.

You may remember what you experienced while you were drifting in trance. As with the dreaming segment of this last induction, when you drift, your subconscious might bring up meaningful images, memories, or sensations. They may relate to your auto-suggestion. Through these images, you can receive guidance from your subconscious. If you feel your drifting experience may have been valuable, make a note of it. Tell yourself to remember, then finish your practice. If you are concerned about forgetting something important, take a moment to write a note to yourself, then go right back into your practice.

The depth scale adds another creative component. Scales help to consciously recognize how your trance is continually shifting in and out of different levels. You may be aware of the cycles occurring in sleep, with periods of dreaming followed by periods of deep sleep. This same cycling happens all day long, when you're alert and aware, and even when you're in hypnosis. Your consciousness is always moving in a kind of wave, rising and falling, shifting inwards and outwards. When you use depth scales, you become aware how you shift throughout your day. You can ask a similar question while you're working, "Where am I on the scale now?" The answer you get may even surprise you. Here's what some students experienced:

"My first number was 70, I thought that was about right. The next number was 50. Then at 35, I decided to just stay there. I liked it."

"At the end I got 08. I was lower than I've been able to go before. I lost touch with my body feeling. I couldn't tell where I started and stopped. I liked it."

"I started out at 25. The second number was 15. Then I have no clue what happened next."

Obviously, this last student went deeper after reaching 15 and drifted out of her normal conscious awareness. The numbers gave her an accurate report of her depth.

You can use the numbers while you are in trance to guide your process. Say for example, you like the way you feel when you are below 40 on the scale. Then, if you are only at 60 after your deepening, you can add another one to take you deeper. Wait until you know you are deep enough to work with your key words or your auto-suggestion effectively. On the other hand, if you're already at 30 when you finish your induction, you might decide you don't need to do any more deepenings. As you gain familiarity, you will sense the difference between a light trance and a deep trance, but having the numbers helps make it more conscious. The more you use the depth scale, the more spontaneous and accurate it becomes.

If you like the quality of the voice with the guided inductions, then practice talking to yourself in the same way. An effective leading voice will shift to a more relaxed, rhythmic quality. Change your voice inside your mind; slow down, emphasize the sound and feeling of the words, breathe with the words you are thinking or speaking aloud. Emphasize or repeat important words. One way to practice the self-talk is to listen to the induction again and repeat the words you hear to yourself, mimicking the way they are spoken. One student commented about being led:

> "I feel as though I went very deeply, very quickly, although I did feel deepest and calmest right at the end. I had an interesting idea in hypnosis that it would be okay to imagine a leader or authority figure reading the suggestions to me and this makes it feel stronger."

You can enjoy the feeling of being guided in your own self-practice by the voice suitable to you. Experiment. See what works. The more you practice talking to yourself hypnotically, the more effective your self-talk will be. In the next chapter you will learn a simple way to drop quickly into trance, building on what you already know.

Chapter 12
A Refreshing Dip into Trance

Before you agree to do anything that might add even the smallest amount of
stress to your life, ask yourself: What is my truest intention? Give
yourself time to let a "yes' resound within you. When it's right,
I guarantee that your entire body will feel it.
Oprah Winfrey

Exercise nine - simple self-hypnosis technique

The following exercise illustrates a simple way to use your ideomotor awareness in trance. Your mind-body connection is always operating and can be accessed. To begin, remember the feeling of something that came easily to you. Perhaps one of the inductions or deepenings you experienced that seemed effortless. You might also remember something else in your life that was very comfortable. The feeling of going easily into something is a very simple way of recognizing when your subconscious is saying, "Yes." Remember and feel the feeling. Then say the word, "Yes" in your mind. You will use that "Yes" feeling in this next exercise. This exercise is adapted from David Cheek (1994).

Exercise nine - simple self-hypnosis technique.
Materials needed - pen or pencil and journal.

Time length: 10 minutes.

You will need a pen for this exercise, and you should be sitting upright in a chair. Read through this exercise first, then practice it for yourself.

1 - Hold one end of your pen by the finger tips of one hand, with the hand resting on your leg or your lap. Allow the pen to dangle down towards the floor, so if your hand relaxed, the pen would fall to the floor.

2 - Then ask this question of your subconscious mind: "Will it be all right for me to experience a brief dip into trance when I drop this pen?" Then let go of your question and wait and see what kind of feeling you get in your body. You know your "Yes" feeling. Compare the feeling to the response you get in your body now. Your feeling may be subtle, but still recognizable. If you get a feeling that's not "Yes", stop this exercise and do it later. This might not be a good time for you to experience trance. You can respect your subconscious mind.

3 - When you get a "Yes" response in your body, then add this thought: "When I am in a helpful state of trance, I would like my fingers to relax and drop this pen. After a brief time, I will awaken feeling fine." There's no need to repeat the suggestion, your subconscious will get it the first time.

4 - Then allow yourself to drift and let your awareness go anywhere it wants. You may become aware of your breathing. Think of a happy place, or even bring to mind a simple self-hypnosis induction. Enjoy yourself and allow your whole body to relax.

5 - At some point the pen will drop, as if by itself. There's nothing you need to consciously do to make it happen.

6 - When you notice the pen has dropped, bring your key words to mind. Then let go and drift.

7 - When you sense you've had enough time in trance to be helpful in some way, open your eyes and reorient yourself to the room around you.

Do the exercise now.

Personal responses

Now take a few moments and answer the following questions:

1 - What are you experiencing now?

2 - What did you enjoy about this exercise?

3 - What was your experience of the pen after you allowed your subconscious to lead?

Discussion

This exercise uses two ideomotor signals. First, the sensation in your body tells you if it's a good time to go into trance. Secondly, when your fingers allow the pen to drop, your subconscious is saying you are in trance. Not only can you attend to what your subconscious is telling you through the ideomotor connection, but you also can tell your subconscious when you want a signal. You can become aware of your ideomotor connection by simply attending to your body. The body signals you in many different ways throughout each day. Hunger, tiredness, tension in your shoulders, and shivers down your spine are all ideomotor signals. If you pay attention to your body, you will be more aware of your subconscious signals. They can be as direct as "Yes" or "No" in response to something you are doing or thinking about.

You can use this simple induction to give yourself small "gifts" of trance in the middle of a busy day. Your subconscious will know how to use these short dips into trance most effectively. Each time you do the simple technique, you will get better at dropping the pen into trance.

Were you surprised when the pen dropped? I enjoy using this technique myself because I'm frequently surprised when the pen drops. Surprise is the conscious response to the experience of not consciously controlling the pen. Of course, you can always go into trance without any "tools", but adding a physical response can strengthen your experience.

Now, after a brief dip and settling into trance, is a good time to check-in with yourself. The next chapter will address where you are and obstacles you may be experiencing.

yes

Chapter 13
Reflecting on Obstacles

We spend most of our time and energy in a kind of horizontal thinking.
We move along the surface of things [but] there are times when we stop.
We sit still. We lose ourselves in a pile of leaves or its memory. We
listen and breezes from a whole other world begin to whisper.
James Carroll

Personal check-in

Now I'd like you to review your progress with self-hypnosis. Take a few moments and answer these questions in your journal:

1. Are there particular induction or deepening techniques that really seem to work well for you?

2. Are there any particular parts of your practice you are having difficulty with?

3. Do you notice any changes in your energy level?

4. Have you noticed any changes in your daily stress or tension levels?

5. Have you noticed any changes in your emotions while practicing or have you experienced unexpected emotions?

6. Have you noticed any changes relating to your specific intentions or goals?

7. How do you know when you are in trance?

Each time you assess where you are with your self-hypnosis practice, you will become more aware of what works for you and what doesn't. Every aspect of the process can be modified to suit your personal needs.

Taking a deeper look at obstacles

Once you find a few effective deepening and induction techniques, stick with them. A favorite induction becomes like a familiar place you go to when you want to feel good. You will begin going into trance as soon as you bring to mind your favorite technique - attending to your breath, imagining a staircase, or remembering your favorite place.

If you are having any difficulties with your self-hypnosis practice, they should be addressed. To really learn self-hypnosis, it has to be enjoyable or you will simply lose interest. Does the idea of practicing sound like work? Then don't call it practice, call it something like, "personal quiet time," "self care," or another phrase that is meaningful to you. If you call it something else, be sure the induction leads you to the experience you want. Self-hypnosis can become exactly what you want it to be. Then you will be more apt to make time for practice.

Here's a student's example of her increasing awareness and experience:

"I did my self hypnosis while I was soaking in the bath tub. It works great. First, one of the exciting things for me is that whenever I start self hypnosis, meditation, Reiki or even when I lay down to go to sleep, I'm aware of my energy vibration. Not only is this really cool to both see and feel but it helps me realize that I haven't quieted or slowed down yet. Then I can work with my energy. Such was the case when I was soaking in the tub. I was counting down and yet my energy was still as high as when I started. So I just said, "Okay, let's slow this down with each step and count." I may or may not be sure if it's slowing down with one or two numbers, but by 7 it's definite. I was never aware of this before and it has sure been a great gift to work with. While I was in the tub, I had to keep counting down; I needed mansion staircases but I eventually did go deep enough to not remember some. No, I did not come back to blowing bubbles with my face under the water and the water did not get cold. I just was pretty excited to 'get there' when at first it seemed to be a struggle."

One common problem people experience is being bothered by disruptions. It is helpful to have a peaceful, quiet moment to do self-hypnosis, but it is not necessary. If you've never experienced trance in a noisy environment, you may not believe you can. Remember, you can use anything you are experiencing as part of your induction into hypnosis, including distractions and noise. Be honest with yourself. Acknowledge, as honestly as you can, what you are experiencing. For instance, I sometimes become annoyed by the sound of a barking dog. I could say to myself, "As I hear the dog barking, I'm going into trance." That is good pacing and leading, but I'm not really being honest with myself. What's really disrupting me at this point are my feelings about the sound. I am feeling annoyed and angry. I will do better to start with the feelings, "I am angry . . . and I'm okay!" Then I would continue, "As I am angry, I'm learning how to let go, relax, and enter into trance." This way I give myself permission to feel what I am feeling -- I validate my subconscious. Then I lead into what I want. Relaxation may not happen immediately, but it eventually will, as I relax and trust the process.

On that note, honestly assess your feelings, emotions, or stress level when you begin your practice. By first checking in with what is happening you validate your subconscious. Then you can move into your practice without resisting what is already happening. This is why the practice form begins with a check-in.

You may also have difficulty letting go into trance if you still fear it in some way. A deeper fear may manifest as a knee-jerk reaction during your practice. You may be settling comfortably into your induction and suddenly find yourself wide awake and alert with your eyes open. You may not even be aware why you're suddenly alert. When this happens, remind yourself, "I'm okay." Then ask, "What was that about?" Quiet your mind again, and see what comes. Even if you don't know what a feeling of fear is about, acknowledging it will help you move on. You can say, "I'm afraid, and I'm okay."

If you still struggle with the idea of control, specifically losing it, then it's important to assess your needs. Tell yourself what you want or need to feel safe, even if your needs are not rational. Then include your feelings as part of your trance experience. For example, "As I relax into trance, I will always be as aware as I need to be. I will always be safe." You can address your basic safety needs without ever needing to face a deeper fear head on.

You may also feel like nothing much is going on when you practice. That's okay. It is still beneficial if you are only relaxing your body and quieting your mind. Even though you feel "normal", you may still be in trance. If you want more concrete experiences of trance, then give yourself suggestions to amplify anything you are experiencing.

For example, if all you experience when you practice is a quietness in your mind and a little buzzing in your arms or legs, then use those sensations. Tell yourself, "With each breath (each induction, number, etc . . .) this quietness becomes more profound." Or, "With each sensation I experience, my trance becomes more meaningful." You can encourage more profound manifestations of trance.

Another way to make your experience more meaningful is to go back and look at your initial expectations about hypnosis. Your expectations may be closely aligned with other personal beliefs. Give yourself suggestions to manifest some of the feelings you expected. Of course, make sure to choose qualities furthering your goals and intentions. If you expected to be unaware during trance, and you're comfortable with the idea, then give yourself suggestions to forget things. Remember, though, for most people, forgetting isn't in alignment with their goals. Being more aware is.

Suppose you had an expectancy to be unable to move in trance. You might have seen this in a movie and it made sense to you. You can use this phenomena in a helpful way. Encourage and suggest partial paralysis, but limit it to a specific area of your body. You could say, "As I go into trance, my right hand will become immobilized. As I start to feel the sensation, or lack of sensation, I will know I'm truly experiencing trance." Working in that direction, you can actually lose the ability to move the hand, a very powerful experience ratifying your trance state. If you alter your body in any way, be sure to tell yourself the sensation will go away any time you truly need to use your body again or when you terminate your trance experience. Creating paralysis or anesthesia can be very helpful for working with chronic pain or preparing for a minor medical procedure. We will look at anaesthesia and pain relief in chapter 19. Next we'll look at more trance phenomena you may already be experiencing.

Chapter 14
The Experience of Trance

Self-worth comes from one thing - thinking that you are worthy.
Wayne Dyer

Manifestations of hypnotic trance

How do you know when you're in a trance? With practice, you will come to recognize your own indicators of trance. They will be personal to you and can help you recognize the trance state. Each person manifests trance differently. The most general answer might be, "When I experience a change." Commonly we recognize we were in a trance afterwards, when we "wake up" and find ourselves in our normal consciousness again. Remember, the waking is also another trance.

Below is a partial list of some of the common manifestations of hypnotic trance. I offer this list to spark your awareness of what you may already be experiencing as well to expand your awareness of what else might be possible.

Many of the phenomena on this list are recognized as indicators of trance depth. The development of anesthesia, for instance, indicates a fairly deep level of trance. However, everything listed here can manifest independently of a hypnotic state. You could manifest anesthesia while your consciousness is otherwise unaltered.

Many of these markers are only recognized after the fact, when normal consciousness returns. Our ability to literally "go somewhere else," allows many of the phenomena of trance to manifest. For example, when I am deep in trance, I often lose my normal sense of hearing. I become absorbed in whatever I'm experiencing and have no idea my sense of hearing has gone silent. Only upon awakening does my hearing return. Then, I experience my environment as though someone is turning up the volume.

Although I've separated the following list into emotional, mental, and physical categories, each phenomenon can have all three components. Analgesia, for example, is a lack of physical pain, affected by where your mental awareness is focused and what emotion you are experiencing. An emotion of peace has both a physical and mental component.

I've also graded each section, beginning with more common experiences and ending with less common, another way of indicating depth. Any sensation on the list can be experienced more profoundly, also indicating greater depth.

Emotional manifestations:

At ease
Neutral or blank
Uninhibited
Tranquil
Strong
Distant
Less self-conscious
Separated from cares and pressures
Euphoric
Empathic
Meaningful
Detached
Self-assured
Self-confident
Empowered
Wise
Compassionate
Forgiving
Unconditionally loved
Merged
Detached or emotionless

As noted, any emotion can become its own trance state. All emotional trances can be sustained. They can be just as strong and real as "normal" reality.

Physical manifestations:

Buzzing
Vibration
Light-headedness
Tingling
Light
Heavy
Disconnected
Numb
Blurred vision
Altered voice
Loosening of sense of body
Flushing of skin
Heart rate altered
Blood pressure altered
Altered breathing rhythm
Altered breathing depth
Increased or decreased salivation
Relaxed muscle tension in any muscle in the body
Spontaneous jerking (This may be connected to the release of physical tension.)
Sluggish
Awkward
Sensation of depth (Though difficult to describe, this can be a distinctly physical experience.)
Catalepsy of limbs, eyes, or face
Slow or nonexistent nerve reactions (Lack of the blink reflex is used as a test of depth.)
Slowed pupil response
Detachment from breath
Slower body movements or responses (Indicative of subconscious dominance.)
Sensation of being incredibly large or incredibly small
Spontaneous body movements (Can either be release of tension or manifestations of subconscious intentions, as with ideomotor movements.)
Bodily sensations voluntarily turned on or off (This phenomena is used to create anesthesia and analgesia, to cultivate sexual arousal, or to work with medical conditions like asthma.)
Analgesia in any area of the body or in whole body
Anesthesia in any area of the body or in whole body

Entire body seems separate

Entire body seems extra active or intense

No sense of boundary between body and not-body

Complete separation from body

Cessation of normal body functions (Heart rate, respiration, digestion and other body processes can be slowed to imperceptible rates.)

Mental manifestations:

Alert

Focused

Curious

Interested

Passive

Absorbed

Sensation of depth (Unlike the physical sensation, can be an awareness of a level of depth.)

Suggestible

Altered time perception (May be sped up, slowed down or nonexistent.)

Totally focused on method of induction, to the exclusion of other things

Hyper -aware of noises, qualities of light, physical sensation, smells or tastes

Unaware of noises, qualities of light, physical sensation, smells or tastes

Automatic and instantaneous responses to suggestion, either internal or external

Hyperacuity

Clarity of purpose and meaning of life, work, family.

Amnesia (We experience this continuously by forgetting meaningless information. Amnesia is functional when we forget something we don't want to remember. Amnesia is nonfunctional when it hinders our ability to be in the world.)

Access to heightened logical abilities or insights

Positive hallucination in any of the senses (Perceiving things that are not there, such as hearing voices, feeling sensations on the skin, or seeing visions or apparitions.)

Negative hallucination in any of the senses (Not perceiving things that are there, such as not seeing someone else in the room and possibly even being able to see "through" them.)

Sense of a presence. (This could be perceived positively, negatively, or neutrally, and may be connected to an emotional shift or healing.)

Access to deeper repressed memories

Inability to retain memories

Extra lucid recall of a past event or emotion

Regression (Refers to a return to a previous psychophysical state, with memories and a vivid perception of past experiences.)

No sense of boundary between I and not-I.

Cessation of association to normal ego structures and mind (Can be experienced as a peak experience, the void, or a spiritual state.)

After reading through the list of manifestations, make a note of any you've experienced. If some of these phenomena seem scary to you, remind yourself that you don't have to experience them; you will only experience what serves you. Also, if you want to achieve more profound experiences, then tell yourself the phenomena you experience are okay. What is experienced in deep trance can be deeply meaningful, even to the point of being a transformative spiritual experience.

Changes you can expect

A dip into trance will often re-energize your body and your mind. This is very useful in the middle of the afternoon, when your body cycle may be in a naturally low place. If you do self-hypnosis practice at that time, allow the feeling of tiredness to lead you down, while remaining aware and guiding the process. Following the natural energy cycle, you will reawaken feeling much more energized. If you practice in the morning you may finish too relaxed. You can purposefully move into an energized state with your awakening. Make your awakening longer and clearly focus on how you will feel the energy as it comes into your body. Allow the energy and move with it as you count up. If you prefer the relaxing feeling that lingers after trance, then practice in the evening. Conversely, at night, keep your awakening very brief, so you can stay relaxed and quiet until you are ready for bed.

After practicing a couple of weeks, you will likely experience positive changes. You may notice a shift in your levels of tension, emotions or physical energy. You will find yourself spontaneously doing things relating to your goal. How these changes manifest may even seem a little mysterious. A fairly common observation would be, "I don't know why, but I just noticed I was feeling better," or, "I didn't respond the way I usually do to that situation." It's important to recognize the progress and changes you experience, even if you don't understand how they happened. You may not think they're related to, or caused by, your self-hypnosis practice. That's okay. When you validate what you are experiencing, you can honestly say you are moving toward your goal. When you observe a positive shift, you could even say, "As I am responding more positively to (a certain situation), I am becoming better. I am changing. I am reaching my goal." Even in your normal state, you can pace and lead, validating the changes you are experiencing. Your subconscious will respond. For example, self-hypnosis students have stated:

> "I've been more in control, and less worried about things. I've also been procrastinating less lately."

> "When I go into public places I tend to get stressed. Lately, that's been changing. I tell myself I'm going to be okay. I don't become totally happy and joyful, but I shift to a better place."

> "If I've had a tense day, I can do self-hypnosis and feel myself relax. So, while I don't have a concrete product that is measurable, it is something."

> "I'm sleeping better."

I recommend a month focused on one intent with a regular practice to see profound changes. I believe this is because we need to live the ideas we are trying to manifest for them to become real. (Of course, this could be a limited belief I am holding on to.) The longer you hold your intention, the more you will see changes. Because of your focus on your goal, you will recognize changes you might have missed before. With self-hypnosis, you focus on one aspect, hold your awareness there, and your reality changes. The changes you experience are exciting, mysterious and powerful. In the next chapter, you will tap into some of this mystery with hand levitation.

Chapter 15
Imagination Becomes Real

Everything you can imagine is real.
Pablo Picasso

Exercise ten - hand levitation

The next exercise will open your awareness to more of the mystery of hypnosis -- hand levitation. Hand levitation uses your physical body, but involves more mental experience since you create a wholly new sensation and response.

Before going through the induction, I'll show you a simple way of experiencing your arm muscles working partially under subconscious control. To begin, hold out one arm in front of you horizontally. Let the wrist hang limp. Let the muscles in the arm and shoulder be as loose and relaxed as possible while still keeping the arm up in a horizontal position. Imagine there's a spring attached to the back of your wrist keeping it up in the air. Let the wrist bob up and down a little, to feel the tension of the spring.

Then take your other hand, and rest the tips of your fingers softly on the forearm just behind the spring. As the fingers rest softly on the back of the arm, the spring will stretch and the arm will move down. Then, let the fingers slip off the arm, allowing the spring to pull the arm back up to where it was. Repeat this process several times. Each time, allow the arm to lightly bounce back up to the original position. With practice, you can experience the arm popping up all on its own. It's not difficult. You perceive the sensations in the muscles of the arm and shoulder, but you don't have to be consciously involved in their action. Remember the sensation. You will use it again with the next exercise, though you will be pulling up to assist the arm in raising. Next, you can do the hand levitation induction and then enjoy a brief trance state.

Exercise ten - hand levitation induction.
Materials needed - journal, auto-suggestion and key words
Time - 20 to 30 minutes.

Read your auto-suggestions first, with an open, receptive mind. Then, read aloud:

Now, (your name), rest your hands on your thighs, on the chair you're sitting on, or on a tabletop in front of you. Position your hands so they're separated, palms down. Breathe a few comfortable, relaxing breaths. Become aware of the sensations in your hands.

Now your subconscious will choose which hand to use for this exercise. Bring to mind the "Yes" feeling in your body. Then, ask your subconscious which hand would like to experience levitation. Let go of your question and allow your body to respond. The body will signal which hand you will use as it manifests more of the "Yes" feeling there. Breathe as you wait. Allow your body to respond, and pay attention. The feeling in your hand may be subtle or strong, but you will notice it.

Once you get a "Yes" response, focus your attention on that hand. Become aware of all the sensations and feelings in the hand, no matter what they might be. You might feel the pressure or the temperature where your hand is touching down. You might feel the air on the top hand. Inside your hand, you may perceive other sensations - blood pulsing, warmth, coolness, or even more subtle muscular sensations. Be aware how you can sense these sensations throughout the hand to the tips of the fingers. As you notice these sensations, allow them to get stronger.

Staying present with what you are experiencing, imagine a feeling of lightness in the hand. You may feel this as a sense of hollowness . . . or emptiness . . . as if the skin of the hand were just a shell. You may also imagine your hand is a balloon, filling up with helium, being pulled up gently from within. Enjoy the feelings of lightness. Add to that feeling by pacing whatever else you are sensing. As you feel other sensations, your hand can become lighter and lighter. It may move on its own.

As you feel the lightness getting more perceptible, reach over with your other hand and lightly pull up on the wrist, just a gentle tug. Then let the fingers slide off the wrist and imagine a string being tied there, going up to a large, bright helium balloon.

Enjoy the extra sense of lightness pulling up gently on your arm. Allow this sensation to lead your arm. Allow the subconscious to take control of your arm as it gets lighter and starts to move. The arm becomes separate from you and has a mind of its own. You may even feel the muscles moving on their own, allowing the arm to truly feel different as the whole arm becomes lighter.

Now, reach over and tug gently on the wrist again. This time, pull it up a little into the air. As you hold it there, allow the sensation of lightness to get stronger. Allow the sensation to move into the muscles in the arm. Feel the arm start to lift on its own. Let those muscles tighten and notice how the pressure shifts from the helping hand to the muscles within the levitating hand. As that happens, you can let go with the other hand and enjoy and allow the feeling of this hand floating in the air.

Breathing easily and naturally, the arm can continue rising on its own, little by little, as if gentle breezes were nudging it upwards. As these sensations continue, imagine there is an attraction between the hand and your face, as if there were large hollow magnets in the hand and the face. Allow the magnetic attraction between the hand and face to slowly become stronger.

Within the feeling of lightness in the hand, there is a strong magnetic pull towards the face.

As you feel and imagine the pull between your hand and face, the magnetic force will gently start pulling the hand toward your face. Still becoming lighter and lighter, the hand moves closer to the face. As this happens, the feeling gets stronger, and you enjoy shifting into trance.

Next, imagine the hand finally touching the face. Then, all the lightness drains away and the arm drops gently back into your lap. As that happens, your whole body will relax and go deeply into trance. When your hand drops down into your lap, let your eyes skip down to the words in bold, "Hand down now" and continue reading.

Until then, you can enjoy the lightness, the feeling of the attraction between the face and the hand, and all other sensations you are experiencing.

What word would describe what you are experiencing now? Add the thought, "As I am feeling (your word) I am going deeper into trance. My hand is becoming lighter and lighter and being pulled towards my face."

Continuing to imagine and allow the sensations you are experiencing. Everything you perceive is leading you into a comfortable connection with yourself.

Now, if you get to the end of this sentence before the hand touches the face, then let your eyes slide up the page to the sentence in bold that starts, "Within the feeling of lightness . . . " and continue reading from there.

Hand down now   (gently turn page and continue . . .)

Relax now, (your name). You've done very well. You are learning how to experience trance very effectively. You're learning how to allow your subconscious to lead your body and mind when it serves you.

Now, (your name) say your keywords to yourself softly.

(keywords)

Enjoy the feeling of your key words without needing to do anything, letting your mind drift comfortably.

Your subconscious is already remembering all the other thoughts and feelings connected with your key words.

You can drift for a few moments more now . . . remembering other positive feelings . . . not needing to do anything more.

(Pause and enjoy your awareness for a few moments.)

From within wherever you are, you are learning about yourself.

You enjoy trance more easily each time you practice self-hypnosis.

In a moment I'm going to count up from One to Five. When I reach Five you will return to your normal awareness. Your arm and your face will be normal. You will remember what you've learned and experienced in this pleasant trance state.

Beginning, counting up to . . .

One. Starting to come out of trance.

Two. Gently becoming more aware and alert . . . coming into your breathing.

Three. More aware and awake now, returning to normal. Beginning to move your fingers and toes.

Four. Almost there, almost completely back.

Five. All the way back to a normal consciousness.

End reading aloud.

Personal responses

While this experience is still fresh in your mind, answer the following questions:

1 - What are you feeling or experiencing now?

2 - Did you enjoy the hand levitation technique?

3 - Did you find it interesting, easy or difficult?

4 - Was it helpful for you? How?

Discussion

Hand levitation can be a fascinating experience as it can only be created by using your imagination and allowing your subconscious to respond. Hypnotic levitation is different than having your arm levitated by something outside you. Muscles are activated in this process. With practice, you can allow yourself to experience the hand and arm as separate from you. The subconscious can control the arm without your conscious involvement. You will still be aware of tension in the muscles, but you don't need to consciously control them.

As I mentioned before, this technique is very effective if you have tension in your body. Hand levitation uses the energy in your body rather than trying to resist it. When the hand finally touches the face, then the arm relaxes, and any extra energy in your body dissipates easily. If you simply wanted to raise your arm, you could do so at any time. But the goal, as with other inductions, is to experience the levitation as a result of the vividness and clarity of your imagination. The arm will raise by itself as you learn to allow your subconscious to lead. Hand levitation takes practice. Experiencing it is also very convincing to the conscious mind. If you need to be convinced, this is a good induction to work with. Remember though, you are not trying to make it happen. As you allow the subconscious to lead, you will have conscious awareness of the movement as it's happening. As you relax, your hand will levitate allowing the trance process to continue. It is different than your normal conscious movement. Next, you will work more with this phenomena and begin bringing in more of your conscious intention.

enjoying

trance

Chapter 16
Self-Trust, Self-Guidance

Life is a creative endeavor. It is active, not passive. We are the yeast that leavens our lives into rich, fully baked loaves. When we experience our lives as flat and lackluster, it is our consciousness that is at fault. We hold the inner key that turns our lives from thankless to fruitful. That key is "Blessing."
Julia Cameron

Exercise eleven - self practice

Next, you will do another self practice using the hand levitation induction as a beginning. If you have physical problems with your arm or shoulder, then imagine you are levitating the arm with the same focus and attention as if you were physically doing it. This time, use your own self-talk and guide yourself through the whole induction. Give yourself time to experience the sensations. Work with the imagery of lightness in the hand. Imagine the mass of the arm draining away as it gets lighter or an imagine energy manifesting inside it. Be creative. If you have trouble allowing the arm to begin to levitate, then give it some help. Often being aware of the arm muscles tightening is perceived as conscious control. It's not. Consider the muscles tightening as another interesting awareness in the arm. Let it happen.

Also, as you do this self-practice, I want you to experience your auto-suggestion while you are in trance. Once you achieve a comfortably deep state of trance, then instruct yourself to read your auto-suggestion. You could say something like this:

> "Now, enjoying your trance, you will allow your eyes to open. You can open your eyes and read the words you've written while staying in trance. In fact, the words you read will take you deeper into a comfortable connection with your subconscious. As you read, allow the words to flow through the conscious mind, enjoying the sound and texture of them, without even needing to consciously engage with the ideas they represent. Your subconscious will know exactly the right way to respond."

After giving yourself permission, open your eyes and read your auto-suggestion. Afterwards, let the eyes close again and let yourself drift. Enjoy all the energy, imagery, and feelings arising in you in response to your auto-suggestion. Then, when you are ready, you can count yourself out of the trance.

Exercise eleven - self practice using hand levitation.
Materials needed - journal, auto-suggestion and key words.
Time needed - variable.

Sit in a comfortable position with your hands resting in front of you and place your auto-suggestion where it's easy to see. Do your self-practice with hand levitation or other inductions you enjoy, and read your auto-suggestion.

Personal responses

While this experience is still fresh in your mind, answer the following questions:

1 - What are you experiencing now?

2 - How was your second experience with the hand levitation induction? Did you find it interesting? Was it easy or difficult? Was it helpful for you? Explain.

3 - Describe your experience of reading your auto-suggestion in trance. Was it easy or difficult? How did it make you feel?

Auto-suggestions in hypnosis

Reading through your auto-suggestion in trance can be a completely new experience, as is opening your eyes in trance. As always, be aware of what you enjoy or dislike about each new experience. You can have your eyes open and engage with the world while you are in trance. You may find other times when you can use this ability. Self-hypnosis can be a very adaptable process, generating any kind of energy or awareness you find valuable.

Reading your auto-suggestion in trance allows your conscious intent to go directly into your subconscious. You may experience it as if someone else who intimately knows your desires is guiding you. In trance, you won't experience your words and ideas as you would reading them in your normal conscious state. You may feel very detached and indifferent towards the words. However, you are still gaining the effect of your auto-suggestion. Your subconscious is attending at a very deep level. In fact, by not having your normal emotional involvement with your words, your intentions go very deep.

On the other hand, your words may evoke more emotions or feelings. When they do, allow yourself to go with your responses. You may even pause reading for a few moments to allow a sensation or an image to flow through your awareness. Any response you have to your auto-suggestion in trance will be coming directly from your subconscious. Allow yourself to go with whatever happens. Then continue reading when you find yourself reoriented to the present. Like a dream, images and feelings arising in trance often don't make any logical sense until you return to your normal waking state. Even then, you may not be able to make sense of them. Trust that your intentions are working beneath the surface. Take notes of your experiences and strengthen the relationship between the conscious and subconscious mind.

Also, feel free to continue reading your auto-suggestion to yourself before your practice sessions. The emotional response you get when you read your auto-suggestion in your normal conscious state can be very satisfying. Read it any time of day when you want a boost or when you want to get back on track. You give yourself an energetic gift and affirmation every time you affirm your intentions. In the next chapter we'll explore how to work with any positive or negative emotion you experience.

trust

yourself

Chapter 17
Weight Loss and Addictions

During [these] periods of relaxation after concentrated intellectual activity, the intuitive mind seems to take over and can produce the sudden clarifying insights which give so much joy and delight.
Fritjof Capra

Emotions and trance

This section on managing your emotions is very crucial if you are wanting to change an addictive behavior or lose weight. For example, you may have been, like many people in our culture, conditioned since early in your childhood to eat when you wanted to feel better. As a child you were rewarded with treats or sweets when you were hurt, angry or sad. You also received the loving attention of a parent when you were fed, which makes the conditioning even stronger. These patterns continue to play out unconsciously as an adult. You may find yourself eating unconsciously, when you are not hungry and without even realizing why. You may not even recognize what emotion triggered the craving for food.

In the past, strong emotions may have surprised you and thrown you off balance. Now, learning to recognize how your awareness shifts througout the day, you are becoming more conscious of emotional changes occurring in your life. Strong emotions are also trance states. If you find yourself feeling a strong emotion, you can count yourself up or down to alter your state of mind to your own preference. You can have more control over your emotions. You can take care of yourself. Simply saying, "I'm okay," while feeling an emotion will start shifting old behavior.

In hypnosis, you can do much more by consciously exploring your emotional states. You always retain the ability to feel the emotions you have, but you can decide when they are appropriate. When it suits you, you can move into hypnosis with the intent to explore and release whatever emotions you were feeling. With your conscious, critical mind more relaxed, you will be able to access deeper insights and understanding of emotions or problems you are experiencing. You will be able to experience them in a safe and healthy way. You will gain a clearer understanding of how these emotions are meaningful to you, how they can be changed, and how you need to respond to them.

Knowing you are okay at a core level and that you can take care of yourself in a healthy way when you are feeling any emotion will change your conditioned behaviors around food, smoking, gambling and other addictions. As I helped clients with weight-loss in my private practice, those who were willing to work on their emotions were the most successful. Emotions are at the core of human struggles. When they take responsibility for this work, they truly become empowered and are able to change their bodies and their lives, sometimes dramatically.

What follows is a simple structure for working with emotions. Read through the entire structure. Then you will have an opportunity to explore an uncomfortable or strong emotion in a safe way.

Working with emotions

Have in mind an emotion you want to focus on. Then:

1. **Induce trance** - Use your regular method for inducing self-hypnosis, reminding yourself that you can always take care of yourself. Take your time. Use as many deepenings as you need to induce a comfortable, relaxed state of trance.
2. **Bring on emotion** - Once in trance, tell yourself, "I want to explore and understand this feeling." Then remember the emotion you're interested in. Vividly remember what you were experiencing when you felt it. Be sure to allow the changes in your body. Allow yourself to feel it. Start acting as if you were feeling it. Say to yourself, "I am feeling . . . " and put a name to it. Strengthen it. The purpose here is to make the emotion real, not just a memory. This will be easier in trance. Feeling your emotion in the present will help you understand it better. The feeling and experience will be much more meaningful than the label you've given it.

If the emotion you choose frightens you, then tell yourself to feel just enough of it to remember it in your body, while still being safe. Tell yourself, "I'm feeling (emotion) and I'm okay. I can take care of myself." You don't ever have to go into an unsafe experience with trance. When you feel some of it, still feeling safe, move on to the next steps. As you learn to take care of yourself, you will be able to feel stronger feelings and still be safe.

3. **Awareness** - Be aware of the changes occurring in your mind, body and heart. Knowing how you process the emotion is important. Does your breathing shift? Do you heat up or cool down? Do you feel tension, discomfort, or strange sensations in your body? Recognize whatever changes in you. Your feelings and responses may remind you of other times you felt the same feeling; that's okay.

4. **Memory** - Allow the feeling to guide you to other times and places. You can be aware of the connections this emotion has to other times in your life. You will be more able to understand what it means to you. As you feel this emotion in your safe, familiar state of trance, you gain control over it. So encourage it to get stronger. It can't hurt you.

5. **Suggestions** - When your emotion is strong, you will consciously recognize all the effects it has on you. For example, you may notice you feel less confident, confused or even younger than you are now. You may notice an underlying fear driving the emotion. As you sense these insights, speak to yourself as you do in self-hypnosis. Speak to the fear or uncomfortable feeling with a soothing suggestion. If you feel younger, then imagine a part of you is younger and needs to hear some comforting words. Speak them to yourself.

    Speak directly to old thoughts or programs you encounter, "Stop! I don't want you anymore!." Then say, "I am in control now. I am okay. I am strong." Give yourself as many strengthening, calming affirmations as you need.

6. **Movement** - Allowing yourself to be with the feeling will take away any power it has over you. Responding to feelings with wisdom and intelligence will heal the past hurt or distress. Very often the intensity or quality of your emotion will shift as you are present with the feeling and soothe yourself with suggestions. Even if your emotion is still strong, move on to the next step.

7. **Diminish emotion** - Give yourself the suggestion to allow your emotion to diminish by bringing to mind a feeling you want to feel. You pace and lead by consciously choosing what you want, "As I'm feeling (emotion, body sensation, etc.) I'm becoming (what you want)." You might bring to mind your safe, comfortable place. Engage all your senses with that place. You might even imagine a wave subsiding inside you as calmness returns. Be aware how you begin to feel better, in your body,

your mind, your whole being. How does your breathing change? Do your shoulders or some other parts of your body relax? Does your mind become calmer?

Take as much time as you need to feel calm and comfortable again. You can take care of yourself. Do another deepening to strengthen your control and safety.

8. **Follow-up suggestions** - As you settle back into a calmer place, give yourself more soothing suggestions. Bring your key words to mind. Remind yourself you are in control now. Your feelings are part of you and are okay. No matter how strong your emotions are, you can take care of yourself.

9. **End trance** - Bring yourself out of trance when finished.

Exercise twelve - working with emotions

Materials needed - An emotion and key words.
Time - 25 minutes.

Now you can go through the whole exercise. Pick a strong emotion you've experienced recently that you would like to understand better. If you are working to change a specific behavior, such as eating, remember a recent time you found yourself doing the negative behavior. Go back in your mind to just before it began. Remember where you were, what you were experiencing, and what you were feeling. That's the feeling you want to explore. If the experience you remember was very loaded emotionally, you may want to choose a different, less threatening feeling to begin with. You don't have to give this feeling a name, just remember your sense of it as you do this exercise. If you feel unsure how to proceed, read through the above process again. If you forget where you are, you can pause where you are and refer to the guidlines on the previous pages.

Do exercise twelve now.

Personal responses

Take a few minutes to answer these questions:

1 - How do you feel now?

2 - To what degree were you able to remember and feel your uncomfortable emotion again?

3 - Did you feel unsafe at any time? If so, how did you take care of yourself?

4 - How did your feelings and memories change as you worked with your emotion in trance?

5 - How do you feel now about your emotion?

6 - Would you change any part of the emotional process to better suit you?

Discussion

The knowledge you've gained from shifting your consciousness in trance will give you more confidence in future emotional situations you may encounter. You will be more aware what is happening in you and be able to take care of yourself. Wherever you are, you can initially pause and take care of yourself. You can pace and lead, "I'm feeling... and I'm okay." You can count yourself down into a more relaxed state or the memory of a safe place. Then, later in trance, you can explore the strong emotion in a safe way. Every time you move into and through an emotion consciously, you learn you are okay at a core level. All emotions are okay and, in fact, a valuable part of you. Experiencing them and allowing them gives you a greater sense of control. Your control comes from being more conscious and aware, not from repressing parts of yourself. You can feel more deeply and you don't have to hurt anyone or yourself. With more self-confidence, you can allow emotions to rise and fall naturally. You can experience emotions that used to control you and gain a better understanding of yourself. Here's an example from one of my students:

"I thought I'd try to work with the frustration I feel at work with my boss. At home, I did self-hypnosis. Then, when I tried to remember the feeling, it seemed so far away and insignificant. It felt like too much work to get uncomfortable again. I guess I didn't want to let go of my relaxing feelings. I waited a bit and counted down again. Then I tried harder to remember what I was feeling, where I was, and imagined it again. The feeling did come back. I felt my chest tightening up and my breathing shifted.

"When my forehead tightened it made my face scrunch up. I felt like a little child, like pounding my fists on something. I actually had a flash of the kitchen in the house where I grew up. It surprised me. The feeling was strong but it was okay. I said my affirmation and started breathing again. The feeling drained away almost right away. Then as I relaxed, I felt some sadness. Again, when I said my affirmation, I felt much better, comforted. I think I drifted then a little. I don't remember exactly where I went.

"Afterwards, when I brought my boss to mind, I felt much calmer. I think it helped to let myself feel and remember. I don't know what the memory was about; it left almost as soon as I saw the kitchen."

Emotions are also messages from your subconscious -- they provide feedback about what are experiencing. If you're in a situation where it's not appropriate to feel an emotion deeply, then promise yourself that you'll explore the feeling when you can give it your full attention. You don't have to let your emotions disrupt your day. Be sure, though, to honor your commitment to yourself. Take the time to revisit your emotion later. Respect the relationship you have with your subconscious.

Working with problems

You can use the same process to explore a difficult issue or a mental problem. (We'll look at physical problems in chapter 19.) In hypnosis, all the resources of your subconscious are more accessible. Whereas you may have exhausted rational or conscious solutions to a problem, the subconscious will often bring a fresh perspective. A feeling arising in trance may lead you to a forgotten bit of information or may lead you to a whole new elegant solution.

When you are in trance, bring to mind your problem. State a clear intent to yourself, something like, "I would like a solution to my problem of . . . " Then let go. Stop trying to solve your problem. Allow your awareness to drift. Enjoy the feeling of trance. When working in trance, you don't have to force a result. Your subconscious will work for you. To aid your letting go, remember a comfortable relaxing memory.

As your mind drifts, your subconscious will be working on your task. Be open to any images, feelings, memories and ideas arising. Don't expect the information you receive from the subconscious to make sense right away. Give it time. See where your experiences lead you. If you attend to the non-logical things you experience, you will move to a different perspective regarding your problem. Some helpful form of information will come.

If, after some time in trance, you don't gain insight about your problem, directly ask the assistance of your subconscious. Give yourself a post-hypnotic suggestion like:

"I am very open and receptive. Within my subconscious lies the best possible solution to the problem confronting me. This problem can be solved perfectly without any conscious interference. My subconscious will work for me and provide any awareness and understanding I need. My subconscious will find a solution to (your problem). I will be open to the solution when it arises."

Then bring yourself out of trance and continue with your day. Your subconscious will provide the answer in some way soon, that day, the next, or shortly thereafter. Your solution will often come when you are engaged in something else and aren't expecting it. When an idea or insight comes to mind, it's up to you to attend to it and take action. The intelligence of the subconscious can provide invaluable assistance to your conscious life. The conscious and subconscious are intimately connected. Learning to allow your subconscious guidance is the key.

Have you ever tried to remember someone's name and have it remain just at the edge of your awareness? If you try and reach for it with your mind, it slips away from you. When you let go and relax, the name often comes "of its own accord." The subconscious works when the conscious mind sets back and relaxes. You can't force your subconscious mind to do anything. You can, however, allow it to perform in a most magnificent way.

While in trance, you can also use your imagination to invite the subconscious intelligence into your conscious mind. When you imagine, your body responds at a subtle, subconscious level. Imagine yourself totally focused on an important task. Envision yourself creatively learning a new skill, producing brilliant ideas, speaking easily from your heart, carrying out your plans, being able to remember so vividly that you feel you are living the experience again, or just feeling great in whatever task you are doing. Imagining yourself living the changes you want helps manifest them. Your auto-suggestion has the same effect on major issues in your life. The subconscious will set in motion anything you actively imagine. Next, you'll explore how you can use trance more consciously throughout your day, even with specific activities.

easier

now

Chapter 18
Trance is a Natural State

No matter how much pressure you feel at work, if you could find ways to relax for at least five minutes every hour, you'd be more productive.
Dr. Joyce Brothers

Working in trance

The hypnotic state can help you do certain activities. Just as you can read while in trance, you can do many other activities. You probably do this all the time without realizing it. For instance, have you gone "elsewhere" while washing dishes, sweeping, or doing some other simple activity? These are spontaneous trances. Your subconscious knows everything it needs to know about the activity you're engaged in. Your conscious mind goes somewhere else. Here's an example how one student started using trance:

"I've been experimenting with my art, working in trance. I think I always went into trance anyhow, but now it is more intentional. I've also put myself into trance, then read my auto-suggestions. When I do that, I can see it manifesting. I spontaneously find myself going in my room and working on my art. I find myself acting "as if"; then I know it's working."

When you start to use trances intentionally, you should first make sure you'll be safe. Consider how much interaction you need with the outside world and how much logical, critical thinking you need. If the task you choose requires too much engagement with the outside world, then you will not stay in trance, nor should you.

You can open your eyes and do things in trance, though this takes a little practice. Keeping your focus inward is the key. Most of us have a tendency to shift our intention outward when we open our eyes. Through the conduit of the eyes, we tend to leave our inner experience. Anytime you're daydreaming, opening the eyes tends to shift you back into the physical environment. The shift back to the present is usually so effective that you forget all about where you just were.

One way to shift more gently to external awareness is to begin extending with senses other than vision. While you're in trance, start attending to the sounds around you or the temperature of the room. Then, when you open your eyes while still in trance, keep your attention on these other senses. Focus on the feeling in your body, your breath, a sound you're hearing, or an emotion, while allowing visual information to pass through your awareness. Keep your attention centered on the experience of the trance itself, which may be multi-sensory or an inner knowing.

Repetitive tasks are perfect opportunities for intentional trance. Repetition actually induces trance. Your awareness loosens and relaxes with each dish dipping into the dishwater or each stroke of the rake over the grass. During these movements you can add the thought, "I'm relaxing and becoming more peaceful." Then bring your key words to mind. Let your imagination respond to those words with other images, thoughts or feelings. Menial tasks don't have to be a waste of precious time; they can be joyful opportunities of release and self-improvement.

The advantage to working in trance is that you have better access to your own subconscious intelligence and potentials. As with imagining situations during self-hypnosis, when you actually are in trance, you will spontaneously perceive new creative solutions to problems you are working on. In trance, you can flow easily through a situation where you would normally experience a struggle between conscious fears and your subconscious intelligence. An example would be if you were being tested for something you knew inside and out but you have still have anxiety about testing. You could induce a trance to relax your conscious mind and your fears while keeping in touch with the information you have learned. As part of your induction, you might imagine yourself at work or in an environment where you use your knowledge, a place where you are comfortable, confident, and alert. Then you would be in an optimal state for taking your test.

You can also move into an energized state with trance. When you're hiking in the woods, exercising, or walking to work, you can give yourself positive suggestions. If you're working on self-confidence, then pace and lead with your actual physical experience. For example "As I feel the blood pumping through my veins, I am feeling more confident. As I see the sunlight and the trees, my heart is filling with love and I am becoming stronger." In active trances, give yourself suggestions to become more aware and alert than normal. For instance, "As my body moves with strength, all my senses are becoming heightened. My energy is flowing." All of your conscious experience can further your intentions and deeper goals.

The energized and sometimes rarified experiences we have in sacred spaces are partly due to self-induced trances. Our intent and focus on things sacred opens us up to viewing the world in that profound way. Inner thoughts combine with external perceptions to induce the sacred trance. Unconsciously, we are leading ourselves into trance, "With each step through this (temple, grove, home, landscape), I am feeling my spiritual essence grow and expand. As I feel this energy within me, I know this is a sacred space." Why not invite your most meaningful awareness and intention into everything you do? If you want to expand your spiritual awareness, you could add intent as you walk to work in the morning, "As I walk, I feel the spirit moving through me . . . "

Natural trances

As you become more familiar with self-hypnosis you will start to notice natural trances occuring during the course of each day. There may be certain times of the day when your attention starts to drift, or perhaps your energy level drops or dips. Conversely, you may also notice times when it's easier to focus and you have more energy. These shifts in body energy and awareness are part of your natural cycles. In sleep, you cycle between deep sleep and dream sleep several times through the course of a night. Daytime is no different; your energy shifts all the time. You can work with these cycles. Any time you feel your orientation to reality shifting, you are moving into a different trance. (Remember, your waking state is also a trance.) Whatever way your energy is moving, you can work with it intentionally. As you move down or up, add a suggestion. Use your keywords to affirm your intentions.

Allowing your subconscious to guide you takes practice. It is easy to get locked into the narrow focus of your conscious mind and ignore the subtle subconscious messages. When you're focused on a conscious task, the feeling of tiredness indicating a shift can be irritating and distracting. You can override the tiredness and continue to work, but maintaining focus is harder and the quality of your work suffers. By ignoring the feeling of tiredness, you are resisting a subconscious message to take care of yourself. Your conscious intentions are important, but letting go of them temporarily and allowing your subconscious to lead you will be helpful. With practice, you can trust your subconscious to guide you and keep your energy at an optimal level.

When you feel a shift, close your eyes, take a deep breath or two and relax. Tell yourself it's okay to relax for a few moments, even if you're busy. Since your subconscious is already guiding you downwards, you will find letting go to be very easy. By allowing this natural downward cycle, you validate your subconscious intelligence. There will be less of a struggle between the conscious and subconscious. If you have time to go deeper, count yourself down, telling yourself you'll use just as much time as is appropriate. Bring your key words to mind and let yourself drift. When you've had enough time resting or "checking out," you can count yourself up again and get back to work with more clarity of mind.

Like taking a short nap, brief midday trances are very satisfying. You will awaken feeling refreshed and energized and possibly have a new perspective on whatever task you were working on. When your body's energies are naturally turning inwards, you will go deeper, more easily than at other, more energetic times. If you have time, you can move into a full practice when you feel you are at a downward turn of your energy cycle.

The following two pages show the flow of awareness as it rises through the course of a day, and also during the practice of self-hypnosis.

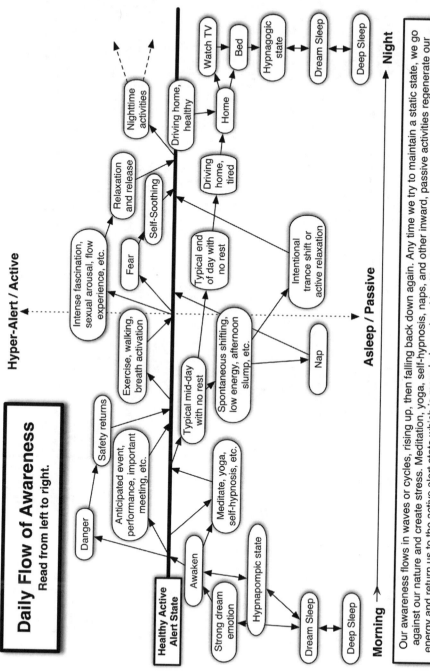

Daily Flow of Awareness
Read from left to right.

Hyper-Alert / Active

Asleep / Passive

Healthy Active Alert State

Danger

Anticipated event, performance, important meeting, etc.

Safety returns

Exercise, walking, breath activation

Intense fascination, sexual arousal, flow experience, etc.

Fear

Relaxation and release

Self-Soothing

Nighttime activities

Driving home, healthy

Watch TV

Bed

Hypnagogic state

Dream Sleep

Deep Sleep

Home

Driving home, tired

Typical end of day with no rest

Intentional trance shift or active relaxation

Typical mid-day with no rest

Spontaneous shifting, low energy, afternoon slump, etc.

Nap

Meditate, yoga, self-hypnosis, etc.

Awaken

Hypnapompic state

Strong dream emotion

Dream Sleep

Deep Sleep

Morning

Night

Our awareness flows in waves or cycles, rising up, then falling back down again. Any time we try to maintain a static state, we go against our nature and create stress. Meditation, yoga, self-hypnosis, naps, and other inward, passive activities regenerate our energy and return us to the active alert state which is more balanced and healthy. Similarly, exercise and engagement activate us and allow us to relax again later. A healthy day will move through the whole cycle several times, from nap to fascination and arousal. If we resist the downward movement, we end up tired, with less energy, flexibility and alertness at the end of the day.

Flowchart, © 2005 - Patrick Marsolek

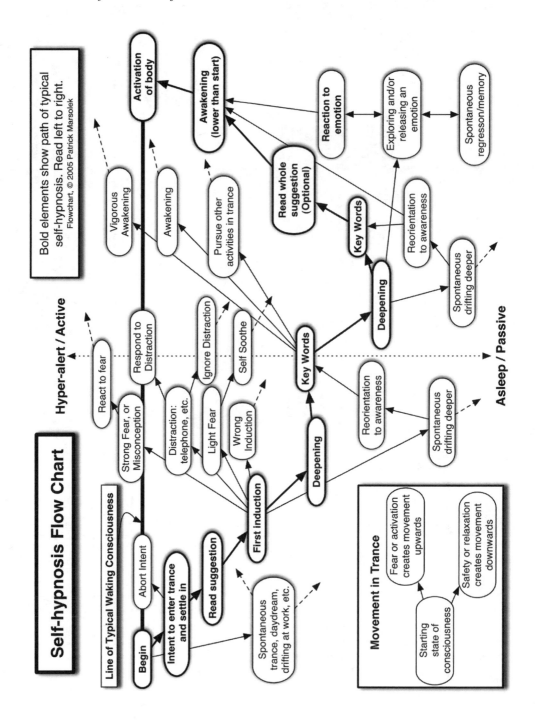

Self-hypnosis Flow Chart

Bold elements show path of typical self-hypnosis. Read left to right.
Flowchart, © 2005 Patrick Marsolek

Hyper-alert / Active

Asleep / Passive

Line of Typical Waking Consciousness

Movement in Trance

Starting state of consciousness

Fear or activation creates movement upwards

Safety or relaxation creates movement downwards

Begin

Abort Intent

Intent to enter trance and settle in

Read suggestion

Spontaneous trance, daydream, drifting at work, etc.

Strong Fear, or Misconception

React to fear

Respond to Distraction

Distraction: telephone, etc.

Ignore Distraction

Light Fear

Self Soothe

Wrong Induction

First induction

Deepening

Key Words

Reorientation to awareness

Spontaneous drifting deeper

Pursue other activities in trance

Awakening

Vigorous Awakening

Activation of body

Awakening (lower than start)

Read whole suggestion (Optional)

Key Words

Deepening

Reorientation to awareness

Spontaneous drifting deeper

Reaction to emotion

Exploring and/or releasing an emotion

Spontaneous regression/memory

Chapter 19
Physical Health and Healing

This art of resting the mind and the power of dismissing from it all care and worry is probably one of the secrets of energy in our great men.
Captain J. A. Hadfield

Pain relief with self-hypnosis

Trance alters the way you interact with your body and can be very effective for relieving pain and discomfort. You will often experience relief from minor discomfort simply by going into trance. This is partly because you are shifting your way of attending, which results in relief. You also are calming and relaxing your body which tends to ease any muscular discomfort you have.

You can go further with pain relief by intentionally creating analgesia and anesthesia in specific parts of the body. Analgesia is an insensitivity to pain and anesthesia is an insensitivity to all sensation. Analgesia is most always preferred over anesthesia since you still have contact with your body. In this section, I will show you a few basic techniques for creating analgesia and anaesthesia to work with pain.

Self-hypnosis also enhances other treatments and healing processes. If you are taking medications, they work better when you're relaxed and comfortable. If you're going through a surgery, you can recover faster using self-hypnosis and you will feel better throughout the whole procedure. Hypnotic intervention for pain can create very positive, tangible results without negative side-effects.

Here's an example from a student of mine:

Dear Patrick,

I have nothing but positive words to share regarding your work with me in hypnotherapy. Before taking your self-hypnosis class, I had been experiencing progressive back and hip pain for nearly two years. I required pain medication or muscle relaxants to sleep and there was not a moment in the day that I was not in pain.

I had changed many of my behaviors in lifting and exercising. I adjusted my posture, joined a health club, and had tried a variety of nontraditional treatments for relief. I finally turned back to traditional medicine and met with an orthopedist. An MRI revealed I have spinal stenosis and a herniated disc. Steroid shots and surgery were my options if the pain did not subside. My office workstation was lowered 5 inches and I received a new chair, which undoubtedly assisted in my recovery, but it was not until I learned about self-hypnosis and the healing that can come from within that I experienced significant pain relief.

In your self-hypnosis class, I first experienced complete pain relief during a guided hypnosis session. Just knowing that a state of relief could be achieved under hypnosis gave me hope that I could eventually reach a pain-free state under normal alertness. I first worked on improving my quality of sleep through self-hypnosis before bed. With your assistance, I then learned to envision a healing energy that may actually repair the damage to my spine.

I am pain free now, and have been for nearly 6 months. I sleep well and I do not take any pain medication for back or hip pain. I am exercising fully, taking care to protect my lower back, and have begun skiing again. I practice self-hypnosis still, especially when I have an occasional flare up of pain. It's good for an overall sense of well-being.

I've become an advocate for self-hypnosis, recognizing how many aspects of our lives can be improved by focusing our attention inward. Hypnotherapy, and teaching people the technique for themselves, should be part of every medical treatment.

Thank you for showing me some of the possibilities for self-improvement.

Sincerely,

Cora

Whatever discomfort you are experiencing, be sure to see a qualified medical professional to diagnose the nature of the pain. Your sensations may be an important message from your body. You may have physical problems that can be addressed and treated by a physician. Also, if you feel there are strong emotional components to your pain, you may want to seek the help of a therapist or hypnotherapist. Working with a person you trust in a safe environment can allow you to work through deeper emotional issues safely and can be a tremendous help with physical issues.

Your experience of pain involves two different components, the sensory and the affective. Physical sensation informs you as to the location and intensity of pain. It may be dull, cold, burning, tingling, aching, continuous or intermittent, tightly focused or spread out. The affective component tells you how much the pain bothers you. These two components may not necessarily correlate. For example, you may welcome the pain of getting a tattoo. The sharp and strong sensations from the needle don't bother you and may even be welcomed as a right of passage. On the other hand, pain from cancer, even when very low in sensation, is frightening and causes a great deal of emotional suffering.

The suffering you experience from pain is affected by your interpretation of it. If pain makes you think of your death, it is likely to cause more suffering. If pain gives you meaning, even if it's intense, it may empower you, as can happen during childbirth or when you are getting a tattoo.

To get a better understanding of the pain you are experiencing, ask yourself these questions: On a scale from 1 to 100, with 100 being the most intense you can imagine, what is the overall intensity of pain you are experiencing now? Allow the first number that comes into mind. This is the sensory component of your pain. Then ask, in general, how bothersome your pain is on a scale from 1 to 100? Again, acknowledge the number. This is the affective component.

You may be surprised at the different numbers you get for each aspect. Just checking in with the scales can help you understand your discomfort better and help you begin to feel better. You can repeat the same questions later after self-hypnosis and observe what changes your experience. Would it be all right for you to have the same sensation in your body while registering a zero on the affective scale? Sensation that doesn't bother you is analgesia.

The ability to physically change your awareness of your body in hypnosis allows you to directly affect the sensory component. You also have the capacity to access deeper beliefs, fears and emotions influencing the affective component. Since self-hypnosis is a treatment residing wholly within you, you will become more self-reliant and less dependent on external support. Even if you have a life threatening illness, you can become stronger and more able to take care of yourself.

When you hypnotically alter your pain, you are affecting the subconscious mechanisms in your body. You can activate or deactivate nerves and pain receptors in your body and brain, change physical characteristics such as heart rate and blood pressure, and alter chemical levels in the blood. You don't need to understand the underlying mechanisms of these changes. By creatively imaging what you want to happen or holding a clear intention, your subconscious intelligence will create the necessary changes in your body.

What follows is a list of several different methods for working with pain. I begin with an emotional, affective technique to help you lessen your immediate sensation so you will relax more and use the deeper, trance techniques. I will explain each technique, then offer a sample script. Use these scripts in conjunction with the other inductions and deepenings you've learned. As with all techniques, be responsive to the emotional connections that rise to the surface. Remember, it's okay to feel, and you can take care of yourself. Releasing an emotional component of pain can be very healing and transform your pain experience.

Scales of discomfort

Create a scale from 1 to 100 to indicate your level of discomfort. Ask inwardly what number describes your pain level and allow your subconscious to respond. You may find it helpful to imagine a blank chalk board in your mind, then allow the number to appear on it. Use both affective and sensory scales for clarity.

Establishing a pain scale will give you better conscious awareness of your changing levels of discomfort. When you register higher numbers, even in the middle of the day, you can pause and take care of yourself. When you register lower numbers, you can be more aware of what allowed you to feel better.

Use discomfort scales before, during and after inductions to help convince your conscious mind.

Script:

> Now ask your subconscious mind what number describes where you are on the scale of discomfort. Allow whatever number comes, even if it's not what you expect. You are developing clear communication with your subconscious.

Describing sensation

For this technique, you will describe, rather than label, the sensation you are experiencing. You will come up with three words to describe this sensation. Allow any and all words that come to mind; they don't have to make sense or be logical. Try to be as honest and accurate as you can with your choice of words. For example, I have a mild pain in my left leg. As I attend to it more, I come up with the words, "pressure, tightness, and throbbing."

After choosing three words, pause a few moments. Breathe. Be present with your feelings. Remind yourself you're okay. Repeat this process several times, each time coming up with three different words. After each group of three words, be with your feelings for a few moments.

This technique works by making you more aware of what you are already experiencing. It brings you into the present. Often, with uncomfortable sensations, you spend most of your time avoiding the experience. Granted, pain is uncomfortable, but by avoiding it, you set up resistance to yourself. If you spend your day avoiding an uncomfortable sensation, you feel worn out and fatigued at bed time.

Emotional aspects of your discomfort will begin to surface through the appearance of affective, descriptive words. For example, the words you choose may be, "sharp, intense, angry." You may also experience a strong feeling of anger. Allow these feelings when they come as they will help release the physical discomfort. Being present with your feelings, even if uncomfortable, will often make you feel better.

As you describe your sensation, you attend to it more. This will cause the sensation to shift. Describing sensations is a good starting point for trance because it will bring some immediate relief to your discomfort, whereby you can relax into other inductions.

Use your pain scales before, during, and after this technique.

Script:

Take a moment now, and attend to the uncomfortable sensation you are experiencing.
I would like you to come up with three different words that describe the sensation.
Take your time with each word.
They don't have to make sense or be logical; just let them come to mind.
See what words come and speak them to yourself.

Now allow yourself to feel and experience what is happening in your body and mind.
Be with the feelings that come in response to the three words.

Repeating the process again, invite three different words to describe what you are experiencing now.

Take your time with each word. Remember they don't have to make sense. All you need
    to do is describe the sensation.
Any emotions that arise are okay. They're part of the process.
In fact, if you wish, you can add this thought whenever you want, "and I'm okay!"
Say the descriptive word, "and I'm okay"

Repeat this process until you experience a shift in the discomfort you are experiencing.
Now you can relax and be more comfortable.

Notice how the sensations in your body or the way you feel about them may have
    changed.
Coming more into touch with what you are feeling will change the nature of your
    discomfort.
Your body will heal and feel more comfortable again as you allow the changes you
    experience.
You can relax more deeply now.

Visualizing sensations and moving them

For this technique, you will imagine how your uncomfortable sensation looks,
sounds, and feels. You will briefly intensify your image of the pain, allowing your sense of
it also to intensify. Then you will allow it to subside. Next, you will move the sensation out
of your body and make it disappear. As the sensation leaves, you will bring to mind your
safe place.

Visualizing the sensation in your body allows you to attend to and engage it more
consciously. You will creatively imagine your discomfort with all senses. Then, as you
begin to move and manipulate your image of the discomfort, you begin to establish some
control. Your creativity will continue guiding you. Having a clear image of your discomfort
makes it much more tangible and accessible. Raising and lowering the intensity gives you a
sense of self-control. Bringing to mind a safe place helps you shift from not wanting a
negative sensation to wanting a positive one.

Script:
    Pay attention to the sensation of the discomfort you are experiencing now.
    Imagine for a moment, if that sensation were to have a color, what color would it be?
    Allow a color to come to mind, whatever feels right to you.

Notice if it's dark or light, pale or bright.

If that sensation were to have a sound, what would it sound like? Imagine hearing the sound it makes.

If the sensation were to have a temperature, how hot or cold would it be? Feel the temperature of your discomfort.

If the sensation were to have a shape, what would it look like? Imagine that shape . . . Imagine feeling it with your hands.

(Use a louder voice)

Now, sensing the color, sound, temperature and shape of your sensation, I want you to imagine, just for a few moments, all these senses getting stronger. Imagine the color getting brighter, the sound getting a little louder, the temperature becoming more intense, and the size of it getting a little bigger.

Imagine it changing, and notice how the sensation you feel also gets a little stronger.

Feel how it is getting stronger. It's okay to feel this sensation right now.

Even though you become more uncomfortable, you are learning about yourself in a very important way.

(Allow your voice to get softer again.)

Now let your sensation return back to where it was.

Let the color, temperature, sound, and size return back to the way they were.

Breathe in a deep breath . . . and exhale all the way.

Allow your sensation to decrease again as you relax.

You can directly affect the sensations you are feeling in your body.

You are gaining control now.

You can change the sensation into one that is much more comfortable to you, more healthy and relaxed.

Now, imagine moving that sensation away from you. It may move toward the back or front, to the side, or even up or down.

Imagine moving the sensation whatever direction is away from you.

Continue breathing easily as you do this, so with each exhale it moves a little further, out and away from your body.

As it begins moving, imagine the color starting to shift, the intensity and brightness of the sensation starting to dim.

Notice how the sound grows quieter. As the sound diminishes, it may even change its tone or frequency.

Notice and imagine how your sensation begins to reduce in size. Notice how the shape begins to shift as it leaves you.

With each breath you breathe, you become more comfortable; as the sensation leaves your body and goes farther and farther away.

All of your perception of this sensation diminshes as you become more comfortable.

Watch it go out away from you towards the most distant place it can go, out to the far edge of your awareness.

Allow it to flow there, quickly or slowly, at a pace that feels right for you.

Watch how, at the end, it disappears completely in a puff of light.

That image disappears.

As the image of the sensation fades away, imagine turning your body around in the opposite direction.

Breathe a sigh of relief.

Bring your safe place to mind and imagine it before you.

Sense and remember all the feelings and sensations of your safe place.

As you move toward your place, allow the feelings to come into your body, especially into any areas where you've been feeling discomfort.

Enjoy your safe place as long as you like, as you are now safe, comfortable and relaxed.

Visualizing and transforming sensations

This technique begins as the last one did. You will imagine how your sensation looks, sounds, feels, and what shape it has. Then you will briefly intensify your senses of it, to understand how you can control it. Afterwards, you will allow that sensation to return to its former state. Then you will creatively transform your perception of your discomfort, allowing it to shift towards healing.

You can allow your subconscious to guide you into the healing or the change you need. For instance, if you imagine the part of your body which is uncomfortable to be a red color, you might ask yourself what a healthy color would be. Wait and allow whatever color comes to mind. Then you can creatively imagine that color coming into that part of your body with the gentle rhythm of your breath. You can also imagine the red color slowly transforming into the right healing color.

In a similar fashion, you can work creatively with any aspect of your body, however you imagine and perceive it. If you have a migraine, you might be aware that it is because the blood vessels are constricted and under pressure. Using your creativity, you can find any number of ways of imaging them returning to a healthy state, being more pliable, relaxed and at ease.

A client of mine, working with endometriosis, asked her subconscious what her body needed. The answer she received was "space." She visualized space inside all the muscles and tissues in and around her womb. Then she imagined space filling up the insides of all her tissues, down to the cellular level. While she imagined this, she experienced an "unwinding" of the tension and discomfort in her body. She also realized there was a need for space in other areas of her life. She imagined herself having emotional in her relationships and felt better.

Your creativity will guide you into what you need. Trust yourself. You don't have to know how to reduce the pressure, only how to imagine it. This is a powerful process.

Script:

Pay attention to the sensation of the discomfort you are experiencing now.

Imagine for a moment, if that sensation were to have a color, what color would it be?

Allow a color to come to mind, whatever feels right to you. Notice if it's dark or light, pale or bright.

If that sensation were to have a sound, what would it sound like? Imagine hearing the sound it makes.

If the sensation were to have a temperature, how hot or cold would it be? Feel the temperature of your discomfort.

If the sensation were to have a shape, what would it look like? Imagine that shape . . . You may even imagine feeling it with your hands.

Now, sensing the color, sound, temperature and shape of your sensation, I want you to imagine, just for a few moments, that all these senses are getting stronger. Imagine the color is getting brighter, the sound getting a little louder, the temperature becoming more intense, and the size of the discomfort getting a little bigger.

Imagine it changing, and notice how the sensation you feel also gets a little stronger. (Use a little louder voice)

Feel how it is getting stronger. It's okay to feel this sensation right now.

Even though you become more uncomfortable, you are learning about yourself in a very important way.

Allow the sensation to return to the way it was.

Breathe easily and comfortably.

Now, however you imagine your sensation or the part of your body that feels discomfort, you can begin working creatively with it.

Using your imagination and intention, you can create a positive change in your body.

Ask yourself, "What does this part of my body need in order to feel better?"

See where this question leads you.

You may get an image of a different color, a movement, a shift in its shape, a nutrient or some kind of energy that's lacking.

Whatever you sense, pay attention. Attend to your subconscious guidance.

You are in a place now where you can creatively give your body anything it needs.

When you sense what you need for healing, you will think of a creative way to take care of yourself.

Use your imagination.

You can bring in any helpers, any elements or forces which would assist you.

You can draw on any wisdom or intelligence that you require.

Feel free to speak to this part of your body as well.

Offer comforting words and phrases.

You can understand how it wants to change.

Allow your body to lead you.

Spend as much time as you need, creatively working and imaging the healing of your discomfort.

Secondary gains

This technique explores possible secondary gains you may be receiving from your discomfort. If you are receiving something in return for your discomfort, like attention or love, your subconscious may not want to let go of the pain, especially if what you receive is perceived as being more important than physical comfort or health. In trance, you can ask if the pain is serving you in some way. You may not think there are any secondary gains to your pain, but, in asking, you allow the subconscious to respond. You will pay attention to the responses you receive and think of alternative, healthier ways to get your needs met.

This is a good technique for everyone to do, even if you don't think you really get any secondary gains, as it deepens your communication with your subconscious.

Script:

Now you will deepen your communication with your subconscious.

You will learn new, effective ways to take care of yourself.

The reason you pay with discomfort is because, at some level, you have not paid attention to other messages.

Since you are sitting here now, present and aware, attending to your experience, you are now paying attention, especially to the deeper levels of awareness.

Say to yourself, "Thank you subconscious for doing your job well . . . Thank you for creating the discomfort I've been experiencing. As I am experiencing (this sensation) I deeply and completely accept myself. Now you've served your purpose. You have my attention. Now you can use your energies to heal the body.

Allow those words to go deep into your subconscious.

Knowing you accept yourself now, deep inside, you can let go of your discomfort.

You have permission to let go.

You may feel emotions coming up as you accept yourself.

Take a moment and allow any emotions or feelings you are experiencing now.

It's okay to let go.

You can attend to the deeper needs inside you. You can take care of yourself physically, mentally, emotionally, and spiritually.

There may be other important needs getting met through your experience of discomfort.

Feeling bad may allow you to receive attention from friends and loved ones or even from yourself.

Since you are now in a positive place to let go of those physical sensations, you can also address the deeper needs you do have, the ones that are important to you.

What deeper needs or wants did you satisfy through the experience of your physical discomfort?

Take some time now and feel the response from your body, your heart and your subconscious.

There may be nothing, but check and see.

Attend to yourself for a few moments. See what comes.

Any secondary gains you have received through your discomfort may be very important to you.

What action can you take now to meet your deeper needs in a healthy way?

You may do something simple - go for a walk, talk to a friend, or pause to breathe more consciously in the middle of your day.

If you need attention and love, you can ask for it now from people who already love and care for you.

Take some time and come up with three things you can do that gives you the same benefit the discomfort did, but in a healthy way.

Be sure what you choose is beneficial to your whole being.

Make sure the things you choose are real, tangible things you can already do, safely and comfortably.

Anytime in the future you feel any degree of discomfort, all you have to do is stop and pay attention to yourself.

You can become aware of your deeper needs, wants, and desires.

Each time you check in, ask the deepest part of yourself what it needs.

Pay attention to the responses you get.

Thank your body and subconscious for getting your attention, for taking care of you.

Each time you pay attention to yourself, you will release more discomfort.

Even now, you can relax and know you are on the healing path.

You are taking care of yourself and getting stronger every day.

Breathe deep and healthy breaths.

Glove anesthesia

With the glove anesthesia technique, you will focus your awareness on your hand, or another comfortable area af your body. You will create anesthesia in the hand through imaging and testing. Then you will transfer the anesthesia to an area of your body experiencing discomfort.

Glove anesthesia can be a very effective tool to create relief from intense or chronic pain. I've also used glove anesthesia successfully to prepare clients for dental work and minor surgeries. This is a technique that takes practice. The more you trust yourself the more effective this technique will be. Also, the deeper you are in trance, the more effective it becomes.

You can test yourself alone or with a helper, to make sure you are experiencing anaesthesia effectively. In the middle of the exercise, when your hand becomes numb, instruct your helper to pinch the skin on the back of the hand. They should do this slowly, being attentive for any signs of discomfort from you. You may feel some pressure or pulling, but you should feel no pain. If you do, deepen yourself again and repeat the exercise for creating numbness in the hand.

  If done correctly, your helper will be able to pinch quite hard and may even leave a welt that will be visible when you come up out of trance. Not everyone will want or need to create physical proof of anesthesia. If you know you're there, you can trust yourself and begin transferring the lack of sensation to other areas in your body. However, having visual proof of your experience can be very helpful for validating your abilities and is quite convincing to the conscious mind.

Script:

  As you relax in a deep and comfortable trance become aware of your hands.

  If you sense one hand is deeper into trance, focus your awareness on that hand.

  Otherwise, ask yourself which hand would like to experience anesthesia.

  Use that hand for this exercise.

  As you become aware of the hand, allow it to rest comfortably.

  You don't have to do anything with the hand.

  Reach over with your other hand and lightly trace a line across the wrist, from one side to the other.

  As you do this, imagine you are placing a healing, numbing band of color across the wrist.

  Feel the sense of that color as it begins soaking down into the muscles of the wrist.

  From there, imagine how with each easy breath, the healing, numbing color begins to flow down into the nerves, muscles and bones of the whole hand, numbing and quieting everything encountered.

  Allow the numbing color to flow all the way out to the tips of your fingers.

  Know that this sensation, or lack of sensation, is healthy and safe and will allow you to take care of yourself in a profound way.

  In addition, imagine sliding this numbed hand into a soft snow bank.

  Hold the hand in the snow and feel the sensation of cold flowing into the hand.

  This sensation meets and merges with the numbing color and both become stronger.

  Holding the hand in the snow, allow the initial wave of tingling to subside as the numbness grows and flows through the hand.

  You can experience the hand becoming numb now.

  As you experience more numbness, imagine the healing color shining brightly inside and through all the nerves, muscles and bones in the hand.

  As conscious awarness departs from the hand, subconscious healing forces take over.

  Imagine and know how every aspect of the hand is returning to its optimal state of health.

Know that you can move any part of your body while staying deeply in trance.

Now, gently reach over with your normal hand and lift the numb hand and move it slowly to a point in your body where you feel discomfort.

Take your time and be gentle and allow the healing numbness in the hand to become stronger as it moves.

Once you place your numb hand on that part of your body, relax again.

Allow the numbness and the color to flow from the hand into the body.

Feel it flowing. Sense and imagine the nerves in the body going through the same process the hand went through, quieting.

Allow the process to continue all by itself.

You don't even have to work at it.

In fact, your mind may drift while your body becomes calm and quiet and the healing numbness flows into your body.

Any discomfort you've been experiencing dissolves away.

You can move your hand to as many other parts as you desire.

Be sure to instruct yourself that the healing sensations can remain in your body as long as is appropriate for you.

When you're finished working with the healing numbness, you can allow your hand to remain wherever you enjoy it. Allow your hand to return to normal as you come out of trance.

Inductions for pain - final thoughts

Once you learn these techniques you can apply them to any pain or discomfort you experience in your life. These techniques are especially valuable in emergency conditions where a calm and clear mind can save you and others from unnecessary suffering. As with any skill, the more you practice, the more effective you become. Combine any of these techniques or alter them to suit you. The scripts are here only to get you started. Be creative. You are only limited by your imagination, which, as you are learning in these exercises, is very real and powerful.

Be sure to go as deep as you need to use these techniques effectively. You might even ask yourself, "How deep do I need to be for this technique to be effective?" See what number comes up. Then, if necessary, do another deepening or two. You can ask the same question for every self-hypnosis practice you do. You do have the essential skills to use the power of your unconscious. The next chapter will discuss how to take what you know and continue applying it to your life.

Chapter 20
Limitless Possibilities

Do not require a description of the countries toward which you sail.
The description does not describe them to you, and tomorrow you
arrive there and know them by inhabiting them.
Ralph Waldo Emerson

Ongoing practice

As you incorporate trance into your daily routine, you will find many other opportunities to shift your awareness and use pacing and leading. Your intentionality and your trance awareness can become an integral aspect of your life, a monitor of personal health and well-being. Any time you feel yourself moving out of balance, you can consciously shift to restore yourself to an optimal state. You'll find yourself flowing in and out of light trances all day long. You've always done this anyway, except now, with the familiarity of trance to guide you, you will do it consciously and be more in sync with the wisdom within.

Be sure to continue with a daily practice schedule. A regular routine will bring balance to your day, keeping you alert and aware while being in touch with deeper feelings and emotions. I encourage you to use the Homework Practice Form. Spending a moment or two consciously reflecting on your experience of trance will help you notice subtle developments in your practice. Also, a daily practice is necessary to manifest your goals. As you use your auto-suggestion for a month, you will see specific changes relating to your intentions.

Your self-hypnosis process can easily blend with any other meditative discipline you already practice. When your mind becomes active while meditating, pace and lead back towards a quiet mind. As your mind becomes calmer, let your self-talk become quiet again. You will find it easier to quiet your mind using self-hypnosis, as you can utilize any distractions, thoughts, or even body sensations as part of the process. With self-hypnosis, you don't have to resist anything, even a busy mind. Any time you utilize what is happening, you're also sending a message to your subconscious that you are okay just as you are. Nothing needs to be different in order to be present with yourself. Your feeling of self-acceptance is the optimal place to move into meditation, because you aren't reaching for something outside of you. In the present, accepting yourself, you can sense the presence of your higher self.

Record your auto-suggestion

Listening to a tape with your own personal auto-suggestion on it can be a tremendously affirming experience. Basking in the light of your personal auto-suggestion is a special gift you can give yourself any time you want to relax, let go, and receive positive, healing energy. You know how to induce trance by yourself, but being able to lie back and receive it also feels great. Here are some basic guidelines for making a tape:

1 - Preparation - Many people find their own voice to be the calmest and safest voice to listen to. If you don't like the sound of your voice, have a trusted friend record the tape for you. Choose which way you want it read, "I am . . ." or "You are . . ." Play some comforting music in the background to help set the mood.

2 - Introduction - Start your tape with suggestions to relax and make yourself comfortable. Loosen any restrictive clothing and unplug the telephone if necessary. Instruct yourself that you will awaken any time a need arises or when you're finished.

3 - Induction and deepening - Guide yourself down through the inductions and deepenings you enjoy. You can repeat one you like, or do two or three separate ones if you want a deeper experience. Approximately ten to fifteen minutes is a good length of time for the induction and deepening phase. As you record this stage, experiment with three kinds of voice - slow, slower and slowest. Let yourself experience the trance while you're recording the tape. Your trance awareness will come through your voice and make it more effective. Talk as though you are actually guiding yourself into trance. Take your time.

4 - Suggestions - Once you have gone as deep as you want to go, read your entire auto-suggestion. Emphasize your keywords and any personal symbols or images you are using. Repeat your keywords several times, before and after your suggestions. You can read your auto-suggestion with an upbeat voice full of enthusiasm and conviction or you can read slowly and calmly in the tone of the induction and deepening. Try it both ways to see which you prefer. Generally, motivational suggestions are given in an upbeat voice. Suggestions aimed at safety and stress reduction are read at a slower and calmer pace. Feel free to improvise and add other soothing words that fit you.

5 - Awakening - Use your normal awakening process at the end. Feel free to incorporate any specific elements you prefer for yourself - dream recall, memory recall, more energy and alertness if you will be listening to your tape in the morning, or continued relaxation if you'll be listening at night.

6 - Listen to the tape and enjoy the process. Allow yourself to let go and receive the full benefits of your intention. If you find yourself noticing things you want to change with your tape, you can do so, but make sure to let go of your critical mind and experience the effects of hypnosis.

If you like being led, then by all means feel free to listen to the guided inductions on the CD any time you want. A familiar induction can calm and relax you when nothing else works. Getting centered again, you can then move easily back into your own practice.

New directions with self-hypnosis

Now you've learned to do self-hypnosis. The tools you need to take care of yourself are within you. You have access to deeper or higher aspects of your consciousness through your connection to your subconscious. You can access your own wisdom and intelligence any time of day, anywhere you are. Granted, we all need connections to others, to our communities and to the natural world. You can rely on your own inner guidance to know when you need to reach out and when you need to reach in for strength and support.

You can also share your trance with others. Let a trusted friend or partner guide you into your inner connection, reading one of the inductions from this manual. Then your auto-suggestion can be read to you while you are in trance. If you have a strong connection with your helper, this can be a deeply profound experience, different than doing your own practice or listening to a tape. Sharing trance together also deepens your connection to each other.

Here are some comments from students who were able to hear their suggestions read back to them:

"It was awesome. Hearing it in a different voice was even more meaningful. It felt like there was more power to my auto-suggestion.

"It was different than when I read my auto-suggestion to myself, and I liked it. I didn't have to come out of trance to enjoy it."

Experiencing trance in a safe, loving environment allows you to go deeper into the most essential and meaningful parts of your being. You might experience your deep connection to the subconscious as a meeting with a person or a special place. You might call this connection a guide, a spirit, soul-essence or God. You can move toward a deeper spiritual connection in trance. Knowing you are connected in a deep, core place inside, you will begin seeing and engaging with your essence in everything you do. Your spiritual essence will manifest in your life.

With self-hypnosis you learn not only how to envision a change, but how to set it into motion, and live it. As you start living the way you want to, your future intentions begin manifesting in the present. In fact, the breath you are breathing now, the thought currently flowing through your mind, and the present movement of your heart may already be transforming you. Can you feel it?

Breathe a moment . . .

Imagine yourself transforming right now.

The next step

Now it's up to you to keep practicing and enjoying self-hypnosis. Practicing is easy when you recognize the benefits of self-hypnosis. After each of the exercises in this manual, I asked the question, "What are you feeling now?" This question puts you in touch with the immediate changes you experience when you practice self-hypnosis. The experience of self-hypnosis itself is stress relieving and relaxing, regardless of the goal or intention you bring to it. Trance makes you feel good. If you recognize how you feel, you will look forward to your practice sessions. Your practice can be just as comfortable and nurturing as taking a bath or getting a massage. You come away feeling better.

Also, since your practice of self-hypnosis is targeted toward a specific part of your life, you will feel positive feelings in that area. You will find it easier to do the things you've been suggesting without needing to think about them. The problem you're focusing on will "mysteriously" become smaller and more manageable. The subconscious creates effortless, exciting changes. Be sure to pay attention to all the changes you experience and validate them. Enjoy them. When you notice something flowing more easily, comment on it, affirm yourself, and lead yourself into your next unfolding. You can use pacing and leading with everything you experience. Anytime you feel some excitement or enthusiasm relating to your goal, pace and lead to more self-empowerment. Emotions are the doorway to the subconscious. Use them.

Also, be sure to act on the insights you receive in trance. If weight loss is your goal, and in trance you see yourself walking happily down the street, recognize the image as guidance from your subconscious. When you finish, go for a walk. Then, while you're walking, pace, lead, and affirm your positive actions. Bring your key words and specific phrases from your auto-suggestion to mind. In trance, you may get new insights how to incorporate your changes, ways that never occurred to you before. Sometimes the message you receive will be loud and clear. One student described it this way:

> "It's a strange feeling, I hear actual words. They're diffferent than my thoughts, clearer. Once, when I first started, there was this rational part saying "This isn't going to work. I'm not going to do this. Then there was this clear voice that came in and said, 'Yes you are.' It didn't feel like the inner conversation with myself; it came from a different source, more clear and stronger."

As you hold your intention, each moment of your life will become exciting. Your transformation will be a wonderful, joyous experience. It still takes work. You must focus and pay attention. You need to practice. Yet, as you enjoy the process, the whole idea of work will become more enjoyable and empowering. You are taking control of your life.

With practice, you will find a comfortable combination of inductions and deepenings that work well for you. Once you fall into a working rhythm, stick to it. Each time you practice, you will get into your comfort zone more quickly and your subconscious will respond faster. You'll find the process proceeding effortlessly, unfolding out of itself. You may not even need to tell yourself what you will be doing, for how long, or what your specific goals are. Your subconscious can take over each time you practice and take you as deep as you need to go.

You do, however, need to continue paying attention to subconscious nudges. A fairly common occurrence in the process of learning self-hypnosis (or any new skill) is to stop practicing once positive changes are felt. We feel better, things are going well, and we let go of the practice. Unfortunately, this usually leaves some old, unwanted behaviors in place. When we get stressed again, we find ourselves falling back into those same patterns. As you feel changes and start improving, make a point of continuing your practice. Keep practicing and keep paying attention to the guidance you receive from your subconscious. When you feel a slump in your energy, pay attention to it. Stop what you are doing and go inwards for a few moments. The little bit of attention you give your subconscious will keep you more balanced and integrated and in a healthier state of mind and body.

Use your affirmations and auto-suggestion

Remember to use your auto-suggestions and affirmations throughout the course of your life. You can continually adapt your daily affirmations to suit your present needs. Adding "I'm okay" to any phrase will help deal with basic safety and comfort issues.

Keep checking in with your feelings. Ask yourself, "What am I feeling now?" Allow a word or two to come. Then ask yourself, "What do I want or need now? What's important to me?" Attend to the answer you receive. Your response may address a physical, mental, or emotional need or a combination of these parts of yourself. Finally, pace and lead with your feelings. Say, "As I am feeling (your words) now, I am becoming (what you want)." Each time you validate what is happening, your subconscious becomes receptive. Your suggestions will lead you into a more positive state.

Your key words can become an automatic reflex in quiet moments, as you are waiting at a stop light or resting between projects. Once you've spent time working with a specific auto-suggestion and its key words, they will always be effective for you. When you bring them to mind, they will trigger a shift. Your breathing will change, your body will relax, your mind will become quieter.

Here's a list of the ways we've used affirmations in this book:

1. Say or think to yourself, "I'm okay." Breathe.

2. Validate feelings, "I'm feeling (your words) and I'm okay."

3. Say or think your key words and let your subconscious respond.

4. Pace and lead with present feelings towards goals and intentions. "As I'm feeling . . . I am becoming . . . "

5. Read your entire auto-suggestion, enjoying the sounds, images and feelings.

6. Use a specific phrase from your auto-suggestion as a daily

affirmation. Change your affirmation each day.

7. Pick one empowering affirmation and read it each night before bed for three or four weeks.

All of these techniques can be used in trance or during your waking state. They are more effective in trance or when you are moving into trance. Pause when you can; take two or three deep breaths. Bring your key words to mind. Better yet, bring any of these techniques to mind when you sense any spontaneous shifting of your awareness, positive or negative. Suppose the clouds part in the middle of a long, dreary day. The sun shines on you for a moment and you feel a wave of happiness. At that moment, your key words can surface. Allow them to resonate through your body. Enjoy the feelings and the connection to yourself.

You can also use your affirmations very effectively in response to any uncomfortable emotion you are feeling. Remember, emotions are also trance states. If you are losing weight or changing an addictive behavior, then use your affirmation when you are feeling drow towards the old behavior. That is the opportune time because your subconscious is listening. Validate what you are feeling; then lead with any positive words right back into a positive feeling. Each time you pace and lead, be honest with what you are experiencing. For example you could say, "I am feeling angry, and I'm becoming healthier . . . " The more honestly you can speak about what you are feeling, the more effective your leading will be. Your subconscious will listen.

Any time you are drifting to sleep, either at night or before a midday nap, bring your key words or a one-line affirmation from your auto-suggestion to mind. Hold that phrase in your mind, repeat it several times as your consciousness starts to drift. This way, you utilize the natural trance of sleep or daydreaming to further your intentions. The last thought you hold in your mind as you shift your state of consciousness will activate your subconscious. This is essentially what you are doing with all your self-hypnosis practice; generating an intent and getting your conscious mind out of the way so your subconscious can respond. Why not use your natural trances too?

After a month of regular practice you will see changes relating to your specific intentions. A month seems to be a good amount of time for your intentions to become seated in the subconscious. You will experience positive changes. Then you can reassess where you are in your life and pick another intention you want to focus on. Go through the whole process of writing and refining your next auto-suggestion. When you write, do the work of imagining, expanding and clarifying your intention. Once you have your new auto-suggestion and key words, bring them into your practice. With this process, you can address whatever life brings you. There are few limitations to what you can accomplish.

You now know the tools you need to experience trance and use it effectively. You know how to induce a state of self-hypnosis, how to deepen it, how to use it effectively, and how to return to your normal state of consciousness. You know how to generate and use effective auto-suggestions, affirmations, and keywords. You know how to apply these basic elements of trance to serve your greater purpose. Your own felt sense of what trance is will guide you into a deeper and more profound connection with your highest potential.

You have the ability to transform yourself. Go for it! You can embrace each new experience, problem or emotion you encounter with appreciation and joy.

Remember, the sky is not the limit.

*A rose opens because she **is** the fragrance she loves.*
Rumi - Translated by Coleman Barks

Appendix A - Definitions of Hypnosis

Hypnosis is a process involving a hypnotist and a subject who agrees to be hypnotized. Being hypnotized is usually characterized by (a) intense concentration, (b) extreme relaxation, and (c) high suggestibility.
- Skeptics Dictionary by Robert Todd Carroll: http://skepdic.com/hypnosis.html

Hypnosis is a naturally occurring altered state of consciousness in which the critical faculty is bypassed (mind in the conscious mode) and acceptable selective thinking established. This simply means that the reasoning, evaluating, judging part of your mind (conscious) is bypassed.
- The TherapistFinder.net Interactive Glossary of Mental Health and Disability Terms written by C. J. Newton

Hypnosis is a state of inner absorption, concentration and focused attention.
- American Society of Clinical Hypnosis web page. http://www.asch.net/

No completely adequate theory of hypnosis has yet been developed, nor can we even establish whether it is a unitary phenomenon or not. Many theories have been proposed, most of them being primarily descriptive rather than explanatory.
- John G. Watkins in Hypnotherapeutic Techniques

Hypnosis is a process that allows us to experience thoughts and images as real.
- David A. Soskis in <u>Teaching Self-hypnosis</u>

Hypnosis may be defined as a sleep-like condition produced by the hypnotist in a subject who allows himself to accept and respond to certain specific suggestions.
- Frank S. Caprio and Joseph R. Berger in <u>Helping Yourself with Self-hypnosis</u>

(Hypnosis is) . . . a complex of two fundamental processes. The first is the construction of a special, temporary orientation to a small range of preoccupations and the second is the relative fading of the generalized reality-orientation into nonfunctional awareness.
- Ronald Shor in "Hypnosis and the concept of the generalized reality-orientation.
   American Journal of Psychotherapy, Vol. 13, 582-602

(Hypnosis is) . . . not a sharply delineated state, but a process along the broad, fluctuating continuum of what is loosely referred to as awareness.
- Willian Kroger in <u>Clinical and Experimental Hypnosis</u>

(Hypnosis is) . . . a state in which the critical mental faculties are temporarily suspended and the person uses mainly imagination or primary process thinking.
- Daniel Araoz in <u>Hypnosis and Sex Therapy</u>

Hypnosis is a controlled dissociated state in which the conscious, critical, intellectual, and logical portion of one's mind is dissociated, inhibited, misdirected, or distracted, allowing for direct access to one's subconscious, thereby making the elicitation of natural and pre-existing subconscious mental mechanisms possible.
- Whitney Hibbard and Raymond Worring in <u>Forensic Hypnosis</u>

Hypnosis is a process that uses our natural ability to go into trance, to access the subconscious and to create positive changes in our lives.
- Patrick Marsolek

Appendix B - Glossary

Affirmation - Positive words or phrases thought or spoken to one's self. Affirmations are useful for repatterning thoughts and beliefs and are highly effective when used in trance.

Amnesia - Partial or total loss of memory.

Arm drop - Induction or deepening technique involving sustained focus on the physical arm held out from the body, and natural muscle fatigue.

Auditory - The sensory modality of hearing. One of three primary sensory modalities through which individuals perceive and interact with the world. Auditory dominant individuals will respond to auditory inductions and will imagine sounds easier. They might say, "That sounds right to me."

Auto-suggestion - A specific, intentional group of ideas which express the manifestation of an intention, written by and for an individual. Similar to an affirmation, but more in-depth and personally tailored to suit an individual's goals and aspirations. Auto-suggestions activate subconscious resources.

Awakening - Any formal or informal process initiating a return to one's normal state of consciousness. Awakenings can be done consciously, subconsciously (as in waking from sleep) or by another person. In some cases, awakening can be a downward movement from a highly energized or euphoric state.

Belief - What is held true, an opinion. In hypnosis, beliefs establish particular viewpoints of reality. A belief is a trance, neither positive nor negative, but a functional way of operating in the world. As with all trances, a person can have an experience outside belief. This may cause distress if there are no ego structures to support the experience. It may also result in a meaningful expansion of awareness.

Catalepsy - A condition in which sensation is lost and the muscles become rigid. This is experienced as an inability to move the muscles.

Conscious mind - The active, dynamic part of a person of which the person is aware. The conscious includes physical, mental, emotional and spiritual aspects and is the seat of the sense of the conscious "I," or ego. The conscious makes up approximately 15% of all a person's functioning.

Deepening - Any formal or informal process which strengthens an altered state, usually moving one's awareness farther from one's normal reality orientation.

Dissociate - To separate from one's normal relationship or connection. One could dissociate from an object or person, a sense, an ego structure, a way of thinking or an orientation to reality. Dissociation induces an altered state.

Envision - To see as if in a vision. To see with absolute clarity with a deep sense of meaning or purpose. Envisioning a desired change furthers the manifestation of that change, especially when practiced in trance.

Eye-Fixation - Induction or deepening technique involving a sustained visual focus on anything objectifiable that brings on natural muscle fatigue.

Future Pacing - A process of envisioning a future scenario with a present awareness, which sets up the probability for the continued awareness in the future. Future pacing sets up an energy pattern in the physical body which makes new behaviors easier to access.

Hyperacuity - An increase in the capacity of the senses.

Hypnagogic - The threshold state experienced while falling asleep when still aware of physical location and normal identity; when dreaming begins.

Hypnopompic - The threshold state experienced when waking from sleep when still in a semi-dream state but aware of physical location and normal identity.

Hypnosis - A process that uses our natural ability to go into trance, to access the subconscious and to create positive changes in our lives.

Hypnotherapist - A trained professional who uses hypnosis and trance to help people with self-improvement and/or for therapeutic purposes.

Ideomotor - An automatic muscular response or movement arising from an idea held in the mind. The movement is not caused consciously and the idea generating the movement may or may not be conscious.

Ideomotor signaling - Subconscious communication bypassing normal conscious filters. As the subconscious and physical body are intimately connected, ideomotor signaling happens continuously and can be perceived by an attentive observer. In hypnosis or self-hypnosis, specific signals can be established which are easier to perceive.

Imagination - The act or power of forming a mind/body construct of senses that are not physically present. The act of imagining activates the body and creates physical responses as if the senses were actually present, including thoughts and feelings.

Induction - Any process of focusing awareness inducing a trance and shifting one's orientation to reality. Inductions can be conscious or subconscious, intentional or spontaneous.

Intention - A meaningful purpose, design or plan. All intention arises out of past experience and moves a person towards the fulfillment of unresolved conscious or subconscious energies.

Kinesthetic - The sensory modality of touch, muscle tension (sensations) and emotions (feelings). One of three primary sensory modalities through which individuals perceive and interact with the world. Kinesthetic dominant individuals will respond to inductions based on feelings and will imagine physical sensations well. They might say, "That feels right to me."

Manifestation - Something revealed or made apparent. In self-hypnosis, manifestation is achieved through the sustained focus on the feeling of the goals' fulfillment.

Pacing - Matching or validating a behavior or experience. In hetero-hypnosis (with another) pacing refers to the way the therapist mirrors the client's behavior to build rapport. In self-hypnosis, the conscious mind paces with manifestations of the subconscious, also building rapport. In both cases, suggestions, direction, or guidance (leading) become more effective when rapport is established.

Pacing and leading - A specific process whereby one acknowledges or validates what is happening and suggests what will happen next. In trance, the connection between the two elements does not have to be logical. This technique also serves as a means of building an association between unrelated phenomena.

Progressive Relaxation - A process of tensing and relaxing various parts of the body to achieve a greater degree of physical relaxation. This technique is effective for relieving physical stress which inhibits trance and thus is an effective hypnotic induction.

Rapport - In close relation, accord, harmony.

Relaxation - A loosening of strictness, severity, focus or force. A condition of looseness, flexibility, and ease.

Regression - A backward movement (through time) of consciousness. In hypnosis, regression is generally seen as a positive act since the subject gains access to earlier, repressed memories and emotions. The backward movement is thought to serve further forward movement, growth and healing. Regression in hypnosis can be full sensory, whereby the client re-experiences an event as if it were happening in the present.

Self-Hypnosis - An intentional, self-induced state of trance, usually for a specific purpose. (See hypnosis.)

State - A particular mental or emotional condition, recognized by objective or subjective phenomena. Though consciousness is continuously in flux, the conscious mind seeks markers to provide reference and orientation. These markers cluster together to become recognizable states of consciousness. States of consciousness are never truly static.

Subconscious mind - The active, dynamic part of a person of which the person is not directly aware. The subconscious mind includes physical, mental, emotional, and spiritual aspects and is the seat of instinct, imagination, emotion, and the physical biological processes of the body, and instinct. The subconscious mind makes up approximately 85% of a person's functioning. It is also the conduit for higher conscious potentials like intuition, healing, and other extended human capacities that are not fully conscious.

Suggestion - To indirectly put a belief, idea, or impulse into the mind.

Trance - An altered state of consciousness in which normal conscious structures are relaxed, shifted or dissolved. The roots of this word refer to a crossing over or a passage.

Unconscious - Not conscious. (See subconscious.)

Visual - The sensory modality of sight. One of three primary sensory modalities through which individuals perceive and interact with the world. Visually dominant individuals will respond to inductions based on images and will imagine visual senses easily. They might say, "That looks right to me."

Appendix C Auto-suggestions

These sample auto-suggestions have been graciously shared by former students of mine. Each one speaks to the needs of an individual person. As you read them, pay attention to your responses. When you encounter a phrase or an idea that doesn't fit, you'll know it. You might even think, "I would have said . . . " When you know certain words don't fit you, write down the correct ones for you. These words will help you recognize what you already know inside and help get your thoughts onto paper. Of course, feel free to use any phrases or words you do like in your own auto-suggestion.

(Thanks to Sandi, Kathy, Art, Veronica, Anne, Mary, George, Lisa, Chris, Pat, Lee Ann, Melanie and Brenda for sharing their auto-suggestions.)

I am quiet water
(self-confidence, trust and healthy pregnancy)

I am a strong woman, confident and powerful.
I am committed to taking care of my body and am very aware of its capabilities.
I float in the quiet water of my own wisdom and strength.

I am quiet water.

My breath and heart are quiet.
My baby can feel the peace and serenity surrounding my body.

I am extremely knowledgeable about my pregnancy.
I am feeling more powerful.
The water surrounds me, nourishes me and protects my baby.

I am quiet water.

My heart is beating quietly as the water envelops me and my baby.
I am the person who decides everything that has to do with my pregnancy and I will do so with confidence, clarity and strength.
My confidence is evident in the way I communicate with others.
I have the ability to make the right decisions for me and my baby.
I am feeling relaxed and confident.

As my confidence flows through me like warm water in the sea, my body works in quiet harmony.
My baby and I feel light as we float in the water of my own wisdom and strength with ease.
I am feeling confident.
I am at peace.
My baby feels safe in me and trusts me.
I feel the overwhelming love and it gives me amazing confidence and a steady, calm, heart and breath.

I am quiet water.

Soft, warm light and calm wisdom
(relaxed and calm)

I feel so relaxed and calm.
All anxiety and worry are washed away by soft, warm, creamy waves of light and love.
I feel cleansed and open to eternal truth from a power greater than myself.
My body, mind, and spirit are immersed in soft, warm, creamy light and

calm wisdom.

I feel so grateful.
I feel so thankful.
I feel so hopeful.
I feel so loved and loving.

I am so relaxed and calm.
All anxiety and worry are washed away by soft, warm, creamy waves of light
and love.
I radiate soft warm loving light and calm wisdom to (family names).
My body, mind, and spirit are immersed in soft, warm,, creamy light and
calm wisdom.

I am so grateful.
I am so thankful.
I am so hopeful.
I am so loved and loving.

I feel so relaxed and calm.
All anxiety and worry are washed away by soft, warm, creamy waves of light
and love.
I feel creative and productive in all aspects of my life.
I feel energized with soft, warm, creamy light and calm wisdom.

I feel so grateful.
I feel so thankful.
I feel so hopeful.
I feel so loved and loving.

I am so relaxed and calm.
All anxiety and worry are washed away by soft, warm, creamy waves of light
and love.
I am cleansed and open to eternal truth from a power greater than myself.
Love and wisdom guide all my choices and feelings.

I am so grateful.
I am so thankful.
I am so hopeful.
I am so loved and loving.

Balance and vitality

I am easily and naturally moving with balance and vitality from the ground of my being.
I am maintaining a comfortable flowing groundedness wherever I go.
I maintain a balance in my being as I move through the day, meeting people, encountering new ideas and energies and I respond with congruence in my own grounded intent.
I easily and naturally integrate my dynamic, moving, grounded self into old thought patterns and energies.
I am strengthening my positive parts and easily discarding old thought patterns.

From within this creative spontaneous present, I am naturally unfolding into new and exciting possibilities.
I am safe and I nourish my being while cultivating a new balance and vitality.
My life is exciting and self-expanding.

A healthy balance comes easily to me.
I am learning to appreciate all my innate skills more and more.
When it's appropriate, I share my gifts with others.
I know I can move within my grounded center.
I know the spirit guided, creative being who always guides me.

I am bringing past learning and insights I have gained into my body.
My deeper soul is wrapped carefully around my heart and body as a caring blanket nurturing me.
This fills me with joy.
I see and know my deepest potentials more each day as past perceived difficulties simply dissolve into new-found light and heartfelt being.

All my joyful becoming brings in abundance to my life at all levels, more love, more insights, and more material satisfaction.
I know I deserve all the gifts I experience as I continue loving, caring and sharing, regenerating spirit in my every step.
In every step, I welcome the guidance of spirit.
I give thanks for the ever-loving support that rises up inside me.
I easily and with utmost inner wisdom, shine the wisdom of spirit out into the world through my being.

I am establishing myself as an artist

I am an artist. I beam when I talk about my creative work. I tell stories through my pictures and my words. As an artist I have the ability to express my ideas, views and emotions in as many different mediums as I choose. I can experiment and explore and share my experiences to show others a different way. I communicate. I am visible. I love what I do.

I am an artist. I exist in a world beyond time when I work with my creativity. I am becoming more relaxed with my day job. As an artist I can be as wild and rebellious as I choose to be. I have the freedom to be different and straying from the norm is encouraged. I continually change and evolve. I am free. I feel fully alive.

I am an artist. I live in multiple worlds at once and cross back and forth. I tap into a vast sea of pure inspiration. I am aware of a multi-dimensional, all encompassing, essence that is alive, intelligent, and available to teach me. I blaze a trail and bring other worlds to this one. I soar. I am having so much fun.

I am an artist. I convey glimpses of the vast unseen world. I am the channel through which the information is sent. I evoke emotion and arouse curiosity in others with my pictures and my words. I show people that the unseen world is vast and there is reason to have hope. I make people think and feel. I encourage others to look past the illusion. I leave a trail. I am fulfilled.

I am an artist.
I am visible.
I am free to soar.
I reveal a trail to the unseen world.

Dancing with joy
(joy & personal strength)

I inhale joy and exhale peace. I am joy. I am love. I am peace.
Joy is my partner in life. I awake with excitement to start a new day. My life is joyful. I enjoy my body awaking slowly. I accept myself and relish whatever state I may be in. Sometimes I am scared, and I am okay. Sometimes I am sad and I am okay. Sometimes I am mad and I am okay. Sometimes I am in the dark and I am okay.

I am inspired to eat fresh foods and drink lots of water. I savor the taste of each bite. I experience my body being replenished with liquids. I stretch and enjoy my body movements. I dance with life, joyfully. I dance in front of the mirror and feel alive. I am proud. I am healthy. I exercise. I love myself.

I am light on my feet. I smile at people on the street. I prance through the day knowing no one can take my joy away. I skip, and run with my shadow. I am on time, because I give myself the time I know I need and deserve. I respect myself and others. I am doing all I can to contribute. My smile is contagious. I bring light to those around me.

With joy, I love my children. I am patient. I am kind. I listen. I play with them. I respect my needs along with theirs. I find creative solutions for conflict. I share their process and teach by example. I slow down to enjoy their magical moments. I hold them and stroke their soft, tender bodies. I enjoy the soft caress of my own body. I am flesh. I am whole. I am one. I feel the breeze upon my skin. I touch the softness of my belly. I feel alive within my own body. I love my sensuality.

I am passionate. I share my joy with my husband. I touch him as I want to be touched. I am open with him and ask him what he wants. I enjoy giving what he asks for. As I experience my joy, I see him more positively. He smiles more. He feels heard. I enjoy each moment we have together. If I am walking away from a problem, I realize it. I give him the time he needs for himself and ask for my needs openly. I feel comfortable with asking him for what I feel I deserve.

As I enjoy the moment, I become clear about what I want. As I enjoy knowing, I am comfortable expressing my desires. As I express myself, I feel confident and proud. I can meet my own needs. I love myself. I love how I evolve in the dance with Joy. I embrace life's challenges as welcome lessons. I feel strong with each embrace. I am dancing in the light and in the darkness.

I enjoy the ying and yang of it all. I am one with the dance of joy. I am clear with my intentions. I am on the path I seek. I am joyful in my fulfillment. I am me and I love. I inhale joy. I exhale release.

As I inhale, I remember joy. As I exhale, I let go.

I am self-confident

I am self-confident.
When I enter a room, I hold my head high and look everyone in the eye.
With each step, I am more confident.
I am safe and in control of myself.
As my emotions flow through each situation, I make decisions that are true to my values.
I am honest, understanding and kind.
I act on my own decisions.

I trust myself and my abilities to handle any situation.
I am safe.
I am in control.
I have the resources and the ability to find the resources.
I feel confident as I look inside myself and inside others for answers.
My values guide all my decisions and actions.
I hold my head high, breathe deeply and speak my heart and mind.

I am visible.
When I speak, I am heard.
I am seen when I enter the room.
I feel safe and confident when I express my feelings.
I am honest with myself and in all situations.
As I speak, I feel love and acceptance for myself.
When I feel, I hold my head high and look everyone in the eye.
I am true to my values.
When I smile, my heart smiles.
I am confident with who I am in every encounter in my life.

All of these ideas are symbolized by three key words: self control, trust and visible.

Joyful writing

I am writing at least one half hour each day and deeply enjoying it.
Each time I write, I tap into my creativity and inspiration.
I tap into this part of myself every day.
My regular practice builds a positive structure for me.
I feel good.
My writing gives me a welcome discipline which channels my creative energy effectively.
I deeply enjoy writing.

I enjoy putting together ideas, connections and insights.
I enjoy communicating my feelings, thoughts and ideas.
My regular daily writing gives me the structure I need to effectively channel my creativity.
My writing allows me to trust myself more deeply, to follow what is right for me.
I know my writing is good.
I know my ideas are good, important, and will be appreciated.
I am a very good writer.

I am very good at communicating my ideas and feelings.
The better I get, the easier I write, the more I learn about myself, the more I truly know.
My writing refines my own sense of who I am and what I am about.
My writing fills me with joy, happiness, creativity and love.
Within the easy discipline that flows from within me, I also stay aware of my body, my heart, and my spirit.
I easily attend to all the needs of my being.
I stretch and walk when I need exercise.
I rest and relax when I need a break.
I eat well and consciously.
I love myself and my wife even more deeply.

From within this easy balance, my creativity flows strong and clear, grounded by spirit, disciplined and filled with vitality.
I write at least one half hour each day and I enjoy it.
Writing fills me with excitement, aliveness, and creativity.
I feel better and better each day.
I am better each and every day.

Joyful writing.

Living in grace

(specific life change)

I am excited to be going to dog training school. I'm confident. I am learning how to successfully support myself doing what I love. I have boundless energy to learn dog training skills and become self-employed. I treasure the time I spend daily learning about dog behavior and training techniques. Each new thing I learn about dog training inspires me to learn another. I am living in grace because I am following my heart. I am focused on creating animal harmony.

I trust I have made the right choice. I am steadfast, unwavering in my commitment to the value of positive dog training. I am encouraged by my strong sense of individuality, my emotional independence. I am thrilled by the sense of transformation I feel, certain I am heading in the right direction. I am exhilarated to be taking concrete steps toward my dog training education and business. Dog training classes are going to be fabulous and I am going to joyfully absorb everything I can. I have plenty of energy to undertake all the necessary preparations for school. I have energy to begin my dog training business and energy to deal with my husband's attitude. Each step I take forward encourages me to take another. I relish each small achievement. I am going to the Dog Academy for the Fall 2005 session. Within six months of finishing training at the Dog Academy, I will be supporting myself, doing what is worthwhile to me. I am living in grace because I am following my heart. I am focused on creating animal harmony.

I am delighted to be making changes. I feel joyous and full of vitality as I make changes. I am fearless in the face of these changes. I am happy and radiant each day. I am at peace with myself because I am living a genuine life. I revel in the freedom to be myself. I savor the brief time I spend daily expanding my intuitive abilities as these help me make changes. As I move toward being self-employed, my relationship and my future with my husband is becoming clear. It will be exactly what it needs to be. When people question my decision, when my husband tries to discourage me, I take a slow, quiet breath, remind myself of this suggestion, and their words just slide away without harm. I am living in grace because I am following my heart. I am focused on creating animal harmony.

I am helping dogs and humans live peacefully, caught together in the splendor of the web of life. I'm enchanted by being able to help animals for a living. I am living in grace. I am creating animal harmony.

I am worthy and self-confident.

Dancing in light
(losing weight and gaining confidence)

I am dancing into a lighter place. I am becoming lighter in my heart and body and I feel great. I am eating a healthy diet and feeling more in control of my life. I am eating only natural foods, including lots of greens and grains. I enjoy the taste of these healthier foods and I feel better eating them. I enjoy knowing I am becoming healthier.

I am physically losing weight as I'm dancing in my own inner lightness. As I feel better, I am drinking lots of water, teas, and juices. Any time I feel uncomfortable feelings, I drink some water, I breathe deeply, and take care of myself in a healthy way. As I'm taking care of myself, I allow myself to feel my emotions. It's okay for me to feel and to let go. I am strong and able to take care of myself emotionally and physically.

I go for short walks every day. I enjoy how my body feels. I enjoy longer walks when I have extra time. I ride my bicycle three times each week. I feel energized and calmed every time I exercise. I am more in my body in a healthy way. I feel better about myself.

I am more confident about my looks. I feel attractive to myself and to others. I am a good person and I know it. I am more fit and full of light. Because I'm more comfortable in my body, I feel more confident meeting people. I know I'm attractive as my inner light shows through my healthy, light body.

I fit into my clothes easier and will easily fit into my old comfortable jeans by my birthday. On that day I will be 25 pounds lighter and I will feel truly comfortable in myself and in my body. This feels so great. My body is more toned and vibrant. I feel confident, excited to be me and to be alive. I am dancing in the light of my being.

All of the healthy changes I'm experiencing make me excited to be alive. I am living my life filled with light, dancing with light, in light. I am eating at regular meal times and enjoying the healthy food I eat. Whenever I eat, I stop when I'm full. When I'm full, I stop, feel satisfied and know I'm in control of myself.

As I become lighter, I am more in control of my life. My friends and family see me in control and feeling better. They see me as I am, filled with light and energy, dancing my life.

I am dancing in light.

I am self-confident

When I enter a room full of musicians, highly educated and/or talented people, I hold my head high, smile and look everyone in the eye.
With each step, I gain control of each part of me.
I am safe and I am in control of me.
As my emotions flow through each situation, I make decisions true to my values.
I am honest, understanding, loving and kind.
I act on my own decisions.

I trust myself and my abilities to handle any situation.
I am safe.
I am in control.
I have the resources and the ability to find the resources.
I feel confident as I look inside myself and others for answers. My values guide all my decisions and actions.
I hold my head high, breathe deeply and speak my heart and mind.

I am visible.
When I speak, I am heard.
I am seen when I enter the room.
I feel safe and confident when I express my feelings.
I am honest with myself in all situations.
As I speak, I feel love and acceptance for myself.
When I feel, I hold my heart high and look everyone in the eye.
I am true to my values.
When I smile, my heart smiles.
I am confident with every personal encounter in my life.

Happy and in control

I am becoming a nonsmoker. This makes me feel good.
I am choosing healthier alternatives to smoking.
When I wish to relax, I listen to a CD, do progressive relaxation or belly breathing. These activities relax me and make me feel more calm and in control.
I feel lighter, calmer, healthier and enjoy knowing I am becoming a healthier person. This makes me very happy.

Any time I have a craving for a cigarette, I drink a glass of cool water and take a deep breath.
The craving dissolves away and I feel more in control.
This makes me happy.
Any discomfort I feel triggers a deep relaxing breath.
I remember I am in control and I can take care of myself.

I now smell better. My breath and my clothes smell much better.
I am much more confident about kissing my husband, knowing I smell good and feel good about myself. This helps our relationship.

Any time I feel uncomfortable in my emotions, I breathe deeply.
I take care of myself in a healthy way.
As I am calm and connected in myself, I can allow emotions and feel good.
I know it's okay for me to feel and let go.
I am strong and able to take care of myself physically and emotionally.

Being a nonsmoker, I am more confident and relaxed around a crowd of people.
I remember my inner strength and abilities.
This feels very good and makes me happy.
I know I can take care of myself.

On my quit date, I will feel confident and aware of what is going on in my body.
I am happy and excited to have made this healthy life change for myself.
I look forward to being a nonsmoker.

Each day I get closer to my quit date, I feel better and better about becoming a nonsmoker.
I am up for the challenge.
I know how good I will feel in my heart, body and mind.
I already have more confidence in myself.
This makes me happy.

I am excited to think about not being controlled by my urges to smoke.
Instead, I know I am in control.

I am drinking lots of fluids and my body is becoming healthier.
My lungs are clearing and I am breathing easily.
I feel proud to be taking such good care of my body.
I am in control.
I am happy.

I am REBORN!

(smoking cessation)

I am becoming a nonsmoker and I feel delight in my body and my soul.
I am in control and allow myself to be okay.
I no longer have a desire for cigarettes.
I feel healthier and happy to be alive.

My sense of taste is returning and I take pleasure in the foods that are nourishing me.
My sense of smell is astounding me with the awesome smell of the fresh crisp air of winter and I am in awe of the smell of refreshing flowers as they bloom in spring.
I am thrilled to be here now.

My lungs are cleansing with every smoke-free breath I take and I feel proud for taking this healing path.
I am becoming a nonsmoker and I feel delight within my body and my soul.
I am in control and allow myself to be okay.

I am cleansing my body by drinking eight glasses of water a day to flush out the toxins in my body.
I am exercising every day and my heart is beating stronger with every fresh breath I take.
I am breathing easier and freer and I feel invigorated.
I am thinking more clearly as the oxygen flows freely through my body into my brain and I feel vibrant.

I enjoy the fresh smell of my skin, breath, and hair.
I am attractive to myself and to those around me and I feel beautiful.
I am becoming a nonsmoker and I feel delight within my body and my soul.
I am in control and allow myself to be okay.

As I am healing the physical part of my being, I am also healing the emotional part of my being by allowing myself to be in touch with my emotions.
It is okay for me to experience my emotions as I feel strong and confident.
I face each emotion with positive reinforcement and feel at peace.

I practice deep breathing exercises when I am anxious and I feel calm.
I practice progressive relaxation techniques when I am stressed and I feel relaxed and re-freshed.
I feel pride in the accomplishments I make each day - one day at a time.

I am becoming a nonsmoker and I feel delight within my body and my soul.
I am in control and allow myself to be okay.

I am REBORN!!

As I breathe

(social anxiety, self-confidence)

As I breathe…I am healed.
Wind brushes through me, cleansing my body of darkness.
My mind, neck, chest, arms, hands, knees and legs are relaxed….
I stand tall and my heart beat remains calm.

As I breathe…I am strong.
I walk with confidence into large crowded rooms, airplanes, schools and stores….
I am safe and sound.
The wind carries me on my journey.

As I breathe…I feel joy and laughter bubble up from within.
I reach out to people with delight and excitement.
Words flow easily and freely,
And I joke around.

As I breathe…I am stronger.
Like the wind across the prairie I allow emotions to come…and go and
I express myself with confidence when I am with a group of people.
I am beautiful and sexy, like a breath of fresh air.

As I breathe…I am closer to spirit,
I speak honestly, and my words are kind and gentle as a breeze….
With each breath I am guided by the light.
The wind carries me on my journey.
I am confident and comfortable with all of me.

Each day I wake with energy and joy, believing in myself.
I face each new task with enthusiasm.

A deep clear pool

(study & intelligence)

I am a deep clear pool. My own knowledge and intelligence flows through a deep pool inside me. In my pool, I absorb information easily and clearly. I retain what I hear, read and learn effortlessly, like a clear pool absorbing and welcoming life.

In class, I am relaxed, calm and attentive. I take notes and listen and allow my own deeper intelligence to absorb what I need to know. I trust myself as I learn. I know I'm fascinated about learning, about growing and following my path. When I take notes, key words from each sentence register deep in my mind. I access my key words easily and effortlessly and remember what I need to know.

I remember easily in class, when I'm testing, or even when I'm using the information I've learned in my life. Every time I read my notes or study my text, the meaning of the words registers deep within me. I understand what I am studying with depth and clarity.

I can discuss what I am learning with ease, because I trust myself deeply. I am intelligent and strong and filled with calm wisdom. Any time I feel any tension or nervousness I take a deep breath, calm my mind and remind myself, "I'm okay! I am intelligence. I trust myself now, more and more." I feel these words reverberate down through my whole being, calming me, balancing me, and calming the deep pool of my being. I am a deep clear pool.

When I am tested on my knowledge, I feel light, strong and confident. I know my material. I have the knowledge I need. Before I begin a test, I calm my mind with a deep breath. I envision the deep clear pool inside myself filled with knowledge and intelligence. I feel this pool radiating through my whole being. Then, with each question I read, I think clearly. I understand the words. I know I am strong and intelligent. This makes me feel so good! I can do this! Any sounds or other distractions that occur while I'm testing just flow through my mind like running water. They remind me of my own deep clear pool.

Any time I encounter a question or an idea I'm not familiar with, I remind myself, "I'm okay. I am intelligent and capable." I set that question aside. I know if I have time, I'll come back to it later. Then, I may even have a fresh perspective and more clarity. I know that trusting myself is the most important thing I'm learning. I feel self-trust right now, in my body, my mind, my heart and spirit. As I trust myself, my own deep clear pool of intelligence grows deeper and expands to fill my whole being.

I am intelligent. I study well and easily. I enjoy what I'm learning and know it serves me on my path through life. I enjoy this path with each new piece of information I learn. My deep clear pool grows deeper every day. As I am more and more calm and confident in my own intelligence, I learn easier and quicker. My memory becomes sharper and more reliable. With ease and peace of mind, I am growing in my intelligence and knowledge every day. I am a deep clear pool.

I am centered

I am centered.
I cannot be pulled or swayed from my path. I love myself.
I am centered.
I am true to myself. My mind, body, and spirit work together.
I trust myself.
I am centered.

My energy is strong; my body is strong.
I am true to my higher self.
I am centered.
I am grounded.
I am connected to my higher self.
This connection makes me strong and confident.
I am centered.

When I am centered, I feel whole and complete.
In my daily life I am connected and feel light and happy, and in love with myself.
I feel all these positive feelings all the way to my core.
When I'm with others, I see their drama and stay centered and calm.
I am compassionate and empathic and I hold my own energy calm and clear.
When I'm with needy people, I take care of myself and maintain a calm, equal energy.
I am centered and whole.

As I live centered, I find it easier to follow my true path.
I am guided by my own balance and center through the course of my life.
I feel in control, calm, strong and balanced.
I know that nothing will pull me from my path.
Any adversity I encounter only serves to make me stronger and to know myself and my path better. I hold and maintain the light; I am the light.
I am centered.

Deep restful sleep

I have deep restful sleep.

Each night, when I go to sleep, I look forward to the calm, peaceful feelings in my body, mind and heart. I know I am sleeping deeply and profoundly each night. My body knows how to sleep, how to let go and relax very deeply. I trust my body and myself more and more. Even now, I can feel the calm assurance of my subconscious. Its intelligence guides me into a deep restful sleep each night.

As night comes, I anticipate the time I get to relax and let go. I turn off the TV earlier and allow myself some calm, contemplative time. I remember the events of my day and the feelings and emotions I experienced. This calms me and quiets my mind. With each memory and feeling I have, I remind myself, "I'm okay. I had a good day. I can relax now." This allows me to let go and relax. I acknowledge any difficult feelings I had, or problems and remind myself, "I always do the best I can. I can relax now." As I do this, I feel a deep source of calmness start to grow inside me. This fills me with a deep confidence and sense of trust in myself. I love this feeling. I love myself more!

I relax and feel my own confidence and trust. Then a warm, sleepy feeling starts to grow in my body. I enjoy and allow this feeling to guide me. This feeling is a welcome friend that is inside me, guiding me into balance and well-being. I allow this feeling to grow as I prepare for sleep. I pause frequently, to feel the feeling in my body. Then, when I climb into bed, I feel so good. I sink comfortably down into its support and safety. I enjoy these feelings and the comfortable heaviness I feel. This feeling grows as my mind starts to drift. I settle down into a comfortable, deep sleep.

There is an intelligence inside me guiding me through the night, into deep and restful sleep. I trust myself, and feel safe, calm and happy. I have deep restful sleep. Any time I awaken during the night, I instantly remember the self trust and safety I feel. I reorient myself to my calm, safe bed and bedroom. I remember the words, "I'm okay. I am safe, calm and re-laxed." These words send a wave of relaxation down through my whole being, calming my mind, body, heart and spirit. Then, as I relax, I feel my body and mind connected and balanced again. If I need to go to the bathroom, I do, enjoying the sleepy feeling returning to my body. I know that in taking care of myself, I will be able to sleep deeper through the rest of the night.

In the morning I awaken feeling refreshed and energized. I allow the positive feelings and the energy in my body to move me out into another beautiful day. I remember how important it is for me to take care of my whole being - body, mind and heart. I give thanks to my subconscious for resting and recharging my being. As I go through the day, the deep rest of the previous night slumbers within me - a part of me looks forward to the next night's restful sleep.

Breath of life
(peace and meditation)

Breath of life.

Every morning I wake up refreshed and energized.
I have a clear mind and feel bright and cheery.

I go downstairs into the kitchen and drink a glass of Living Water.
I feel the flow of life vibrate through my being.

I settle into the solarium and sit for 15 minutes.
I breathe with intentional attention.
In breath, out breath, no breath.
I let thoughts pass like a gentle breeze through the aspens.

I am at peace and connected to the source, allowing the Well-Being.
I access all of everything I desire and it is given to me.

In this space I am the real (name) and I know it.
I am who I really am.

Breath of life.

Deep blue sigh

(stress and tension)

I am a deep blue sigh. Ahhhh . . . .
With each breath I take, the deep blue color of wisdom and being flows into my body, mind
and heart. I breathe . . . and relax right now.
Ahhhh . . . I am a deep blue sigh.

In my deepest, quietest, and most balanced self I have a deep blue source that is my center.
I am a calm wisdom and strength in my core. With each breath I breathe, I remember this
connection inside me. I learn about it each day as a source of my strength and balance.
With this source I am transforming my life. I am learning how to take care of myself and my
energy. I am staying balanced and calm, feeling my own deep blue sigh.

Any time I feel any tension in my body I remember my own inner connection. I take a deep
breath, close my eyes for a moment, and sigh inwardly and outwardly. I dissolve away all
the tension in that breath and remember who I am becoming now. Any time I sense my mind
starting to race, I remember the thought, "Deep blue sigh . . . I'm okay right now!" Then I
breathe, let my shoulders drop, and allow my face to relax and smooth out.
I am a deep blue sigh. Ahhhh . . . .

As I smooth out each time, I am more in touch with my heart. I know I am okay just the way
I am. I feel my body. I am in touch with my body. I massage any tension I feel in my face,
my neck or in my arms or legs. As I rub myself, I remember the words, "Deep blue sigh." I
settle down into my own inner wisdom.

I feel so good doing this. A new energy and vitality is coming into my being. At work, I am
calmer, clearer and more focused. My calmness sends deep blue out to the others around
me. My whole environment feels friendlier and happier. I am happier now.

I feel so much better when I come home at the end of the day. I am much more loving with
my family. I enjoy being with my family. As I am more comfortable and relaxed with myself. I feel my own deep blue sigh calming and connecting my whole family. We enjoy
sharing time with each other.

Any time I feel pressure building inside me, I give myself extra time to remember my deep
blue sigh. At work, I pause what I'm doing, close my eyes and become aware of my breathing. Then, I remember the deep blue color I know and trust. I imagine the color flowing into
my body, directly into my solar plexus where I feel the pressure. As soon as I do this, I feel

a change. My body relaxes. My mind relaxes. My whole being remembers I am okay. I am in control in a healthy way. I can relax now.
I am a deep blue sigh. Ahhhh . . . .

Then, as I become calm and balanced again. I can address the workload I have. As I am calm, I think clear and sharp. I take care of myself. I ask for help when I need it. I know I can say "No." when I need to. I do good work and I take care of myself. As I am a deep blue sigh, I am working better. I am more focused. I am much better to be around. I love myself more and I feel great.
I am a deep blue sigh. Ahhhh . . . .

I am confident and comfortable with all of me

When I am face to face with a client, I am relaxed, free and creative.
I remain balanced, centered and at peace listening to my inner flow.
I am confident and comfortable.

I embrace whatever the client brings into the session.
I join with the client, confident I can contain the client's pain, fear, anger and anxiety.
I am confident and comfortable.

With each breath, I breathe confidence and energy into each cell of my body.
I am talented, intelligent and insightful.
All I need to know is within me.
I am confident and comfortable with all of me.

Appendix D - Scripts

Some of these scripts are variations of the ones in this book; they have been altered to fit general use. They can be adapted as inductions and deepenings. As always, feel free to change any script to suit your specific needs.

Suggestibility

To begin, I'd like you to sit upright in a comfortable chair so you can breathe deeply and easily.

As you sit comfortably, take a deep breath in . . . and exhale all the way out.

Do this again, nice deep breath in . . . and out.

Now I'd like you to extend both your arms straight out in front of you with your palms facing down.

If you can't do this, then just imagine your arms are out in front of you.

Close your eyes and continue breathing easily and naturally and listen to the sound of my voice.

I'd like you to imagine the handle of a thick, plastic bucket just beneath your left hand.

Let your hand close around the handle.

Then imagine someone turning on a faucet just above the bucket and letting a stream of water flow into the bucket, starting to fill it up.

You may see the bucket and the flowing water in your mind's eye.

You may feel its weight beginning to pull your hand down . . . and you may also hear the sound of the water splashing into the bucket.

Enjoy these senses however you imagine them.

As you do this, your whole arm will start to get heavy.

You can allow that feeling; you don't have to resist it.

Your arm may even begin to move in response.

At the same time, I want you to imagine that there's a string looped around the palm of your right hand.

This string goes up to a bright helium balloon that's filling up, getting larger and larger, pulling your hand up gently.

However you imagine this, enjoy it.

You may even see the color of the balloon getting brighter.

What color is it?

You may feel the string pulling up stronger on your hand.

You may hear the sound of the balloon expanding as the helium rushes in.

With each breath you breathe . . . easily and naturally . . . imagine the bucket with the water getting heavier and heavier.

Imagine the balloon getting lighter and lighter.

Allow and enjoy all these sensations.

You can allow your feelings to flow into your body.

You don't have to resist anything you're experiencing.

You can allow your hands and arms to move as they want.

You can hear the sounds . . . feel the feelings in your hands, arms, and shoulders . . . and see those images more and more clearly.

Enjoy these sensations for a few more moments.

Then, allowing those senses to stay with you, I'd like you to open your eyes and notice where your hands and arms are now.

Then let go of the images and allow your arms to drop down into your lap.

Let your body return to normal.

Body relaxation with counting

In a few moments, I'm going to begin counting slowly from ten down to one.

As I count, you will feel your body relax again, and you will return to a comfortable, light trance state.

As each number drifts by, you can hear another part of your mind repeating the number, like an echo . . . relaxing you.

You may also see the number drift through your inner vision, taking you into a more comfortable place.

The deeper you go, the more comfortable and safe you become.

At the count of one you will settle into a light trance state.

As I count you down, allow each number to coincide with your exhaling breath, taking you deeper. Every time you see and hear a number, you can allow whatever breath you have in your body to flow easily out of you, relaxing you . . . and you can say the number with the end of your breath.

So, beginning now with . . . .

Ten . . . exhaling.

Letting go . . . hearing the number echo inside inside your mind, allowing all muscles of your face to loosen up and relax . . . and spreading through your eyes, your nose and mouth . . . your jaw.

Nine . . . a relaxing calmness easing down through all the muscles in your neck.

Eight . . . and down into all the muscles and nerves in your shoulders . . . more and more relaxed, deeper and deeper.

Seven . . . down . . . drifting through your chest and upper back, deeply and comfortably.

Six . . . echoing softly inside and spreading into your upper arms.

Five . . . flowing down with each sinking breath into your forearms, into your hands and all the way out the tips of your fingers.

Four . . . continuing . . . flowing down through the center of your body, into your abdomen and lower back, deeper and calmer.

Three . . . letting the relaxation spread down through your pelvis and your groin, front and back, flowing down into your legs, and your knees.

Two . . . flowing down through your lower legs, all the way down to your feet and the tips of your toes.

One . . . all the way down, much deeper, letting your whole body relax deeply, melting away any remaining tension and smoothing out, deeper and completely relaxed.

That's good, feeling just right inside, more and more comfortable, safe and relaxed.

Safe place with senses

In a moment, I want you to imagine a special place.

As you sense and imagine this place, you will go deeper into trance in a way that's just right for you.

And as you drift now, you may remember a very pleasant place, a place where you can feel safe, comfortable, and relaxed.

This might be a real place or an imaginary place, whatever feels right to you.

You might be inside or out, with friends or alone . . . trust your deeper self to guide you.

Let your body memory guide you into the feeling, the memory that you know is just right for you.

Enjoy the feelings and memories of this safe comfortable place.

Engage all your senses in the experience of this place.

See, feel, smell, taste, listen.

Enjoying all your senses, you become safer, calmer and more comfortable right now.

The feelings of this safe place pervade your whole being.

Allow yourself to drift into and through all these sensations, going deeper, becoming more comfortable and more relaxed.

Eye-fixation

To begin, find a comfortable position.

If at any time you need to move, you can do so.

You can always take care of yourself.

Now, you can relax . . . breathe comfortably . . . and listen.

You don't need to force anything . . . You can let things happen as they occur.

If you are lying down, focus your gaze at a spot on the ceiling.

If you are sitting up, focus on a spot on the opposite wall.

If you are not wearing your glasses and your vision is blurry, it's okay to focus on a shape or color.

Pick a spot a little higher up to create some tension in the muscles in your eyes.

Focus your gaze and your awareness on the spot you've chosen.

As you focus, allow your breathing to flow in and out . . . easily and naturally.

You may find your eyes wander from time to time, but they can always return to that spot.

As you focus on your spot . . . you'll find that all other thoughts and sensations coming into your awareness will just pass right through . . . like clouds drifting by on a sunny day.

And gradually you will start to notice changes.

The muscles in and around your eyes may begin to feel a little fatigued; they may tingle or vibrate softly.

Your vision may start to shift or change. Your peripheral vision may shift. The colors you perceive may shift and your focus may change.

Your breathing may slow down more comfortably.

The longer you focus, the more things will start to change.

This is a natural process.

You can allow these changes as they happen.

The longer you focus, you will feel the muscles around your eyes becoming tired and heavy.

And you might imagine how at some point, when the eyes want to close all by themselves, they will do so.

When they close, you can let go of any tension in your body and relax deeply.

Until then, enjoy any sensations you experience, as your eyes become heavier and heavier.

The longer you focus, the more heavy the eyes become.

So heavy . . . they will want to blink if they haven't already.

They can blink as much as they like.

Letting everything happen . . . just as it wants to happen.

As you let everything in your mind, body, heart and spirit please itself, even letting the blinks become slower and bigger.

The eyelids getting very, very heavy and tired . . . . they will want to close.

When they do, you can go down deeply . . . into a pleasant relaxed state.

Until then, just notice and enjoy how heavy and tired they become, how each blink seems to get heavier all by itself, pulling you down into a more comfortable, relaxed state.

When the eyes decide the time is right, they will close by themselves, closing down firmly and comfortably, taking you down with them . . . deeper and deeper.

Letting go is so easy and comfortable. It's so easy just to let your experience happen all

by itself.
You are drifting further and further away.
It is really so very simple and easy.
You need not do anything . . . or try not to do anything.
You are feeling very good in every way.
You are safe, secure and comfortable.
The deeper you go, the better you feel, and the better you feel, the deeper you go.
And now, becoming more relaxed, it doesn't even matter any more what the eyes are
    doing, closed or open . . . no matter. They will close when they're ready, if they're
    not closed already.

Silent period

In a moment, I am going to stop talking to you for two minutes (or "a few moments")
    so you can have some time to take yourself deeper.
You do this by allowing whatever feelings you're experiencing to guide you.
Sensations or feelings may become more profound, and pervade your whole body.
Whatever you are experiencing, allow it to increase and take yourself deeper.
The deeper you go, the better you feel; the better you feel, the more your subconscious
    guides you and the deeper you go.
You let go and let it happen.
After this short period of time, you will feel much deeper and more relaxed.
You will be able to continue in whatever way feels right.
Enjoy.

Progressive relaxation

First, find a relaxed position, preferably lying down or sitting comfortably.
As you relax and settle down, allow your breathing to fall into a comfortable rhythm,
    not too fast, not too slow.
In a few moments, you will tighten and hold tension in different muscle groups in your
    body. You will hold the tension in your muscles firmly without straining yourself.

Then, when you let go of the muscles, you can let go and relax completely.

To begin, tighten all the muscles in your feet. Let your feet curl up as the muscles tighten. Feel the pressure and tension . . . hold it . . . then let go.
Relax completely. Let all the muscles in the feet relax.
Breathe easily and naturally.
One more time now, tighten all the muscles in your feet.
Tense every muscle you can . . . hold that tension.
Let it go. Let all the muscles relax. Enjoy the release of letting go.
Breathe easily and comfortably.

Next, tighten all the muscles in your lower legs and ankles. Parts of the feet may tighten again too. That's okay. Hold the tension.
Now let go, let all the muscles relax and smooth out.
Breathe easily.
Again, tighten all the muscles in your lower legs and ankles. Hold that tension . . . . then let go.
Let all those muscles smooth out and relax.
Breathe easily and naturally.

Now tighten the muscles in your upper legs, knees and buttocks. Let your body move if it needs to. Tighten all those large muscles. Hold the tension . . . then let go.
Let all those muscles relax and smooth out. Let all the tension drain away.
Breathe easily and peacefully.
Again, tighten all the muscles in the upper legs, knees, and buttocks. Front and back, inside and out. Hold that tension . . . then let them go.
Let all the tension drain away. Relax completely.
Breathe easily and comfortably.
Be aware of the sensations in your legs now. You can remember the feeling of deep relaxation.
Notice how the muscles feel.
Breathe comfortably.

Now we'll continue, moving up the body.
Tighten all the muscles in your lower torso, lower abdomen, back, and buttocks. Tighten them all. Inside and out. Let your body move if it needs to. Hold them tight . . . then let them go.

All the muscles are relaxing and letting go. Allow all the tension to drain away. This feels so good.

Breathe easily and comfortably.

Again, tighten the lower part of your body, all the muscles, inside and out, back and front, everything. Holding . . . then let them all go and relax.

Let all the tension drain away now.

Breathe easily and smoothly.

Moving up to the chest and the upper back, tighten all the muscles you can in your chest and shoulders, front and back, even into the neck. Tense your upper body. Hold that tension . . . then relax.

Let all the tension drain away. Relax all those muscles.

Breathe more and more easily.

Again, tighten all the muscles in your upper chest, shoulders, front and back, sides, and up into the neck. Holding . . . feeling the tension . . . then let go.

Let them all go. Relax completely, let all the tension drain away.

And breathe easily and naturally.

Now move to your hands. Tense and tighten all the muscles in your hands. Make a fist, tense your wrists and forearms. Tense the end of your arm and hands. Holding tight, clenching . . . then let go.

Let all the muscles relax, and allow the tension to drain away.

Breathe easily and comfortably.

Again, make a fist with your hand, wrist and forearm. Allow all the muscles to tighten, building the tension.

You may even get some vibration in the arm from the tension.

Then let go, let all the tension drain away.

Breathe easily and smoothly.

Next, moving to the upper arms. Tighten all the muscles, in your elbow, upper arm and shoulders. Your elbow may even bend. Hold all those muscles tight.

Then let go, let them all relax and release . . . let all the tension flow out of your body.

Breathing easily and more relaxed.

Again, tighten the muscles of the upper arm, shoulders and elbow. Allow all those muscles to tense and tighten . . . hold that tension . . . then let it go.

Let all the muscles relax. They can smooth out and relax now.

Breathe easily in and out.

Now, moving up to the head, neck and face. Tighten all the muscles in your face, tightening the neck and jaw. The shoulders may move; that's okay. All holding, scrunching . . . then let go and relax.

Release all the tension.

Breathe easily and comfortably, letting go.

One more time, tighten all the muscles in your face, jaw and neck, holding all those muscles, scrunching. Feeling all the tension . . . holding it . . . then let go.

Let all the muscles relax now, and breathe easily and comfortably.

As you breathe now, easily, you feel so good, relaxed all over.

Be aware what you are feeling in your body.

This is the feeling of your relaxation.

Breathe in and out comfortably.

Enjoy your felt sense of relaxation.

Enjoy the deep peace in you.

Your body is relaxed now.

Bring your key words to mind and enjoy yourself.

Any time you want, you can repeat this process, going through your whole body.

You can repeat any areas still feeling tense or tight.

You can take care of yourself.

And now, you can energize yourself enough to bring yourself up to a normal state of consciousness.

Descending stairs

Imagine now in your mind's eye a staircase unlike any you've ever seen before.

It's as if this staircase were in a misty cloud floating or suspended in midair, and you are standing at the head of this staircase.

You look down and know there are twenty special stairs.

These stairs are carpeted in a thick plush carpet of your favorite color.

See the color.

Imagine you are standing in your bare feet.

Feel the thick, plush carpet between your toes.

On one side, also going down the stairs, is a firm, wooden banister.

You can place your hand on the banister and feel its support.

In a moment we are going to move comfortably down these stairs . . . from the twentieth
　down to the first.
With each step down, you will go deeper and deeper, into a relaxed comfortable trance.
When you reach the first step, you will be twice as deep as you are now.

Beginning now, stepping down to,
Twenty.
Deeper relaxed.
Breathing easily and naturally
Nineteen.
Feeling the carpet, the railing, and the feeling of going deeper.
Your body remembers.
Eighteen.
Deeper relaxed.
Seventeen.
With each step, letting go and getting easier.
Sixteen.
Your mind may even drift.
Enjoy yourself.
Fifteen.
Feels so good.
Fourteen.
Feeling the sensation of dropping down.
Thirteen.
More comfortable and calm
Twelve.
Eleven.
Ten.
Halfway down.
Enjoying everything happening as it happens.
Nine.
More and more deeply relaxed, spreading through your whole body.
Eight.
So easy and natural.
Seven.
Six.
Five.

So deep, your own connection getting clearer and stronger.
Four.
More profoundly safe and comfortable with each step.
Three.
Almost there.
Two.
Letting go now.
One.
All the way down, so deep and comfortable.
Even now, still settling down and going deeper.
You trust yourself more and more.

Closed door

Now, wherever you are, I want you to look off to your side and notice there's a large, wooden door.
You can move towards the door, noticing it also has a fascinating, brass doorknob.
As you approach the door, pause in front of it.
In a moment you are going to open that door and go through.
On the other side is a place you can go and feel completely safe, comfortable and alive.
You may not even know what that place will be.
It may be a real place or an imaginary place.
Your subconscious knows it to be the perfect place for you now.
It is already creating all the feelings and senses you need in that place to best serve your deepest intentions.
You might even feel curious . . . enjoy that feeling.
Now you can open that door.
Then move forward and go through the door.
Enjoy everything you experience.
Wherever you find yourself now, allow and engage with all the feelings and sensations that arise within you.
You have no worries or responsibilities.
You can enjoy yourself completely.
As you let go, and go deeper into this place, you go deeper into trance.
You are as safe and comfortable and alive as you need to be.

Appendix E - Bibliography

This is a brief list of the books I have found most valuable professionally and in my own self-hypnosis practice. These are not all available new, but can be obtained through Inter-library loans. If you are interested in delving deeper into hypnosis, there are many more books on hypnosis and self-hypnosis as well as abundant information on the Internet. Also included in this list are articles referenced in the text.

Acosta, Judith and Prager, Judith Simon (2002). The Worst is Over: Verbal First Aid to Calm, Relieve Pain, Promote Healing and Save Lives. San Diego: Jodere.

Anbar, R.D. and Hall, H.R. (2004). "Self-hypnosis for Habit Cough." In The Journal of Pediatry, Feb, vol.144 no. 2, pp. 213-7.

Araoz, Daniel L. (1982). Hypnosis and Sex Therapy. New York: Brunner/Mazel.

Barber, Joseph (1996). Hypnosis & Suggestion in the Treatment of Pain: A Clinical Guide, W.W. Norton & Co.

Bates, Betsy (2001). "Self-hypnosis Controls Nervous Habits and Tics." In Pediatric News, Oct, 2001 vol. 35 no. 10, p.28.

Cheek, David B. (1994). Hypnosis: The Application of Ideomotor Techniques. Boston: Allyn and Bacon.

Churchill, Randal (1997). Become the Dream: The Transforming Power of Hypnotic Dream-work. Transforming Press.

Dossey, Larry (2000). "Hypnosis: A Window into the Soul of Healing." In Alternative Therapies, vol. 6 no. 2, pp. 102-11.

Durbin, Paul G. (1998). Kissing Frogs: The Practical Uses of Hypnotherapy. Dubuque: Kendall/Hunt Publishing.

Edgette, John H. and Edgette, Janet Sason (1995). Handbook of Hypnotic Phenomena in Psychotherapy. New York: Brunner/Mazel.

Erickson, Milton and Rossi, Ernest (1981). Experiencing Hypnosis: Therapeutic Approaches to Altered States. New York: Irvington Publishers.

Erickson, Milton; Rossi, Ernest; and Rossi, Sheila (1976). Hypnotic Realities. New York: Irvington Publishers.

Fain, Jean (2004). "You Are Getting Thinner: Close Your Eyes . . ." In O, The Oprah Magazine, August, 2004 vol. 5 no. 8, p.176(4).

Hadley, Josie and Staudacher, Carol (1989). Hypnosis for Change. Oakland: New Harbinger Publications.

Hammond, D. Corydon (1990). Handbook of Hypnotic Suggestions & Metaphors. New York: W.W. Norton & Co.

Hammond, D. Corydon (2001). "Treatment of Chronic Fatigue with Neurofeedback and Self-hypnosis." In NeuroRehabilitation, vol. 16 no. 4, pp. 295–300.

Hibbard, Whitney and Worring, Raymond (1996). Forensic Hypnosis. Springfield: Charles C. Thomas.

Hogan, K. and LaBay, M. (2000). Through the Open Door: Secrets of Self-Hypnosis. Pelican Publishing.

Laidlaw, Tannis M. and Willett, Michael J. (2002). "Self-hypnosis Tapes for Anxious Cancer Patients: An Evaluation Using Personalized Emotional Index (PEI) Diary Data." In Contemporary Hypnosis, vol. 19, no.1, pp. 25–33.

Lang, Elvira et al. (2000). "Adjunctive Non-pharmacological Analgesia for Invasive Medical Procedures: A Randomized Trial." In The Lancet, April 29, vol. 355 no. 9214, p.1486.

Lecron, Leslie (1970) <u>Self-Hypnotism: The Technique and Its Use in Daily Living.</u> Signet.

Mavromatis, Andreas (1987). <u>Hypnagogia: The Unique State of Consciousness between Wakefulness and Sleep</u>. London: Routledge.

Nickelson, Connie et al. (1999). "What if Your Patient Prefers an Alternative Pain Control Method? Self-hypnosis in the Control of Pain." In <u>Southern Medical Journal</u>, vol. 92, no. 5.

Patterson, David R. (2004). "Treating Pain with Hypnosis." In <u>Current Directions in Psychological Science</u>, vol. 13 no. 6, p. 252.

Price, Scarlet (2005). "Hypnosis: Practical use in Rehabilitation." In <u>Healthcare Review</u>, vol.18 no. 2, p.4(1).

Rossi, Ernest L., and Cheek, David B. (1994). <u>Mind-Body Therapy: Methods of Ideodynamic Healing in Hypnosis</u>. New York : W.W. Norton & Co.

Soskis, David A. (1986). <u>Teaching Self-Hypnosis: An Introductory Guide for Clinicians.</u> New York: W.W. Norton.

The Times. (United Kingdom), "Trance helps students pass exams." Jun 04, 2001.

The Times. (United Kingdom), "Self-hypnosis can provide a low-risk environment in which to build confidence and develop our optimism." Jan 29, 2005.

The Times. (United Kingdom), "Study shows hypnosis can lessen stress and trauma associated with medical examinations." Jan 24, 2005.

"Total relaxation aids natural childbirth: hypnobirthing prepares mentally and physically." (Reader Question). In <u>Patient Education Management</u>, Feb 2002 vol. 9 no. 2, p.22(2).

Watkins, John G. (1986). <u>Hypnotherapeutic Techniques: The Practice of Clinical Hypnosis</u>, Vol. 1. New York; Irvington Publishers.

Appendix F - Binaural Beat Frequencies

The CD included with this manual uses binaural beat frequencies. Binaural beats are internal auditory responses which result from the interaction of two different sounds in opposite ears. For example, if a tone of 400 Hz (Hertz) is heard in the right ear and a tone of 410 Hz is heard simultaneously in the left ear, the difference between the two tones, 10 Hz, is perceived in the brain.

Binaural beats were discovered in 1839 by a German experimenter, H. W. Dove. Due to the distance between each ear, we hear incoming sounds slightly out of sync. Our brains have learned how to process this subtle information and tell us where the sound is coming from. This allows us to locate the source of a sound very accurately. Though we aren't sound locating when listening on headphones, the brain still entrains to the frequencies.

The reason binaural beat frequencies are used in this recording is because the low end of our hearing is around 30 Hz; humans are not able to hear lower than about 30 Hz. There are low tones on each track of the CD generating binaural beat frequencies between 5 and 15 Hz. These are the frequencies associated with the alpha and theta brain wave states. While you listen to the CD, your brain follows the auditory stimulus and generates the same lower frequencies in your brain. The alpha and theta brain wave states are conducive to relaxation, accessing inner creative states and working with the subconscious.

As these tones help you have the experience of these altered states of consciousness, you will find it easier to recreate them in your own practice. You will never become reliant on the binaural tones to create these frequencies in your brain, because they are a natural part of your physiology and consciousness. Also, whether or not you enter into the lower brain wave states is always up to you. The sound frequencies never force you to do anything. They only make it easier for you to go where you want to go.

The Monroe Institute has spent over 30 years researching binaural beat frequencies and their effect on the brain. See www.monroeinstitute.org for more information and research on binaural beat frequencies.

Index

transform

yourself

Give the gift of *Transform Yourself* to your friends and colleagues.

Check Your Local Bookstore or Order Here

◊ **YES,** I want _____ copies of *TRANSFORM YOURSELF: a self-hypnosis manual* (with audio CD) for $27.00 each.

◊ **YES,** I am interested in having Patrick Marsolek speak or give a seminar to my company, association, school or organization. Please send me information.

Include $4.00 shipping and handling for one book, and $2.00 for each additional book. Canadian orders must include payment in US funds, with 7% GST added. Payment must accompany orders. Allow 3 weeks for delivery.

My check or money order for $_____ is enclosed.

Please charge my ◊ Visa ◊ Mastercard ◊ American Express

Name_____

Organization_____

Address_____

City/State/Zip_____

Phone_____E-mail_____

Card #_____

Exp. Date_____‚_____Name on Card_____

Call (406) 443-3439
Make your checks payable and return to:

Inner Workings Resources
P.O. Box 1264
Helena, MT 59624

www.innerworkingsresources.com
Fax: (406) 442-9120

2855